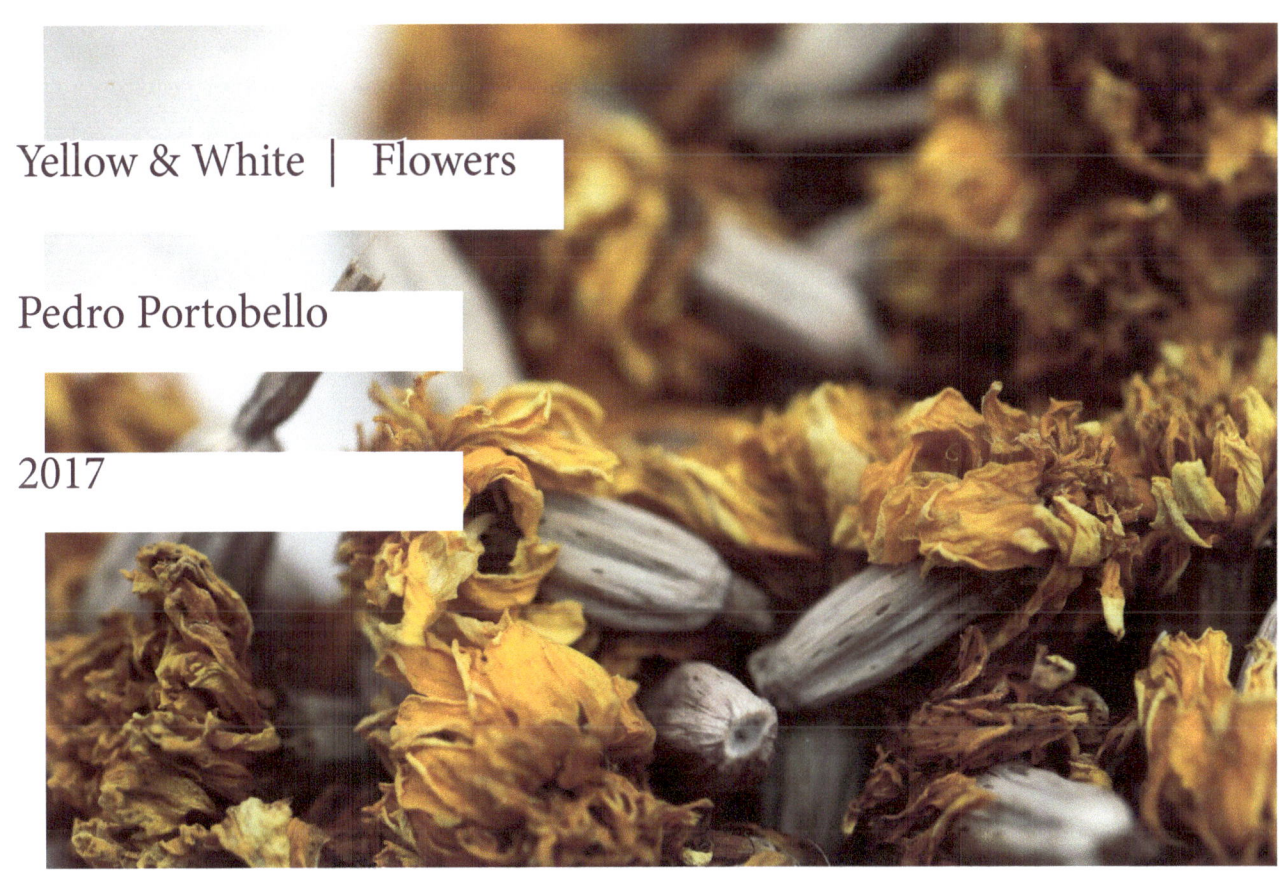

Yellow & White | Flowers

Pedro Portobello

2017

Pedro Portobello was born in Lobito, Angola, in 1958.

He obtained his Ph.D. in Communication Sciences (2005) and degrees in Journalism (1999) and Law (1981) at the University of Coimbra.

He is a Professor at the Instituto Superior Miguel Torga (Coimbra), and led the Degree in Social Communication course until 2017.

He is also a Visiting Professor at the Institute of Information Sciences and Administration (Iscia - Aveiro), a Consultant in Communication for the Port of Aveiro (APA) and the Portuguese Ports Association (APP).

Formerly a journalist for portuguese publications and stations "TSF", "Expresso", "Grande Reportagem", "TVI", "Tal & Qual" and the "Jornal de Coimbra", Dinis still undertakes work as a photo-journalist.

He is also the author of several photography exhibitions and websites, accessible through dmareport.blogspot.pt

As a deputy in the Portuguese Parliament (Socialist Party), Dinis worked in partnership with Jaime Ramos (Social Democrat Party) to sponsor the first project to create local radio stations in Portugal (1983).

He has over two dozen books and photo albums published.

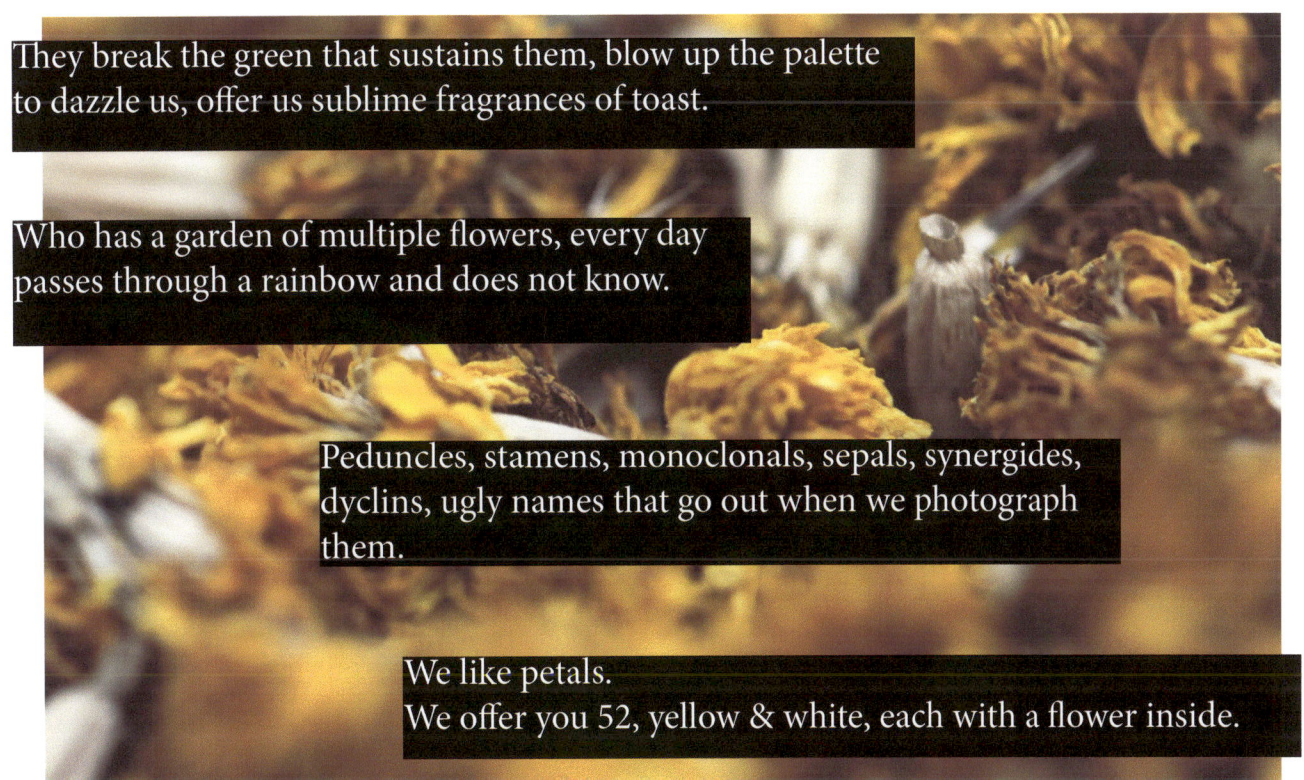

They break the green that sustains them, blow up the palette to dazzle us, offer us sublime fragrances of toast.

Who has a garden of multiple flowers, every day passes through a rainbow and does not know.

Peduncles, stamens, monoclonals, sepals, synergides, dyclins, ugly names that go out when we photograph them.

We like petals.
We offer you 52, yellow & white, each with a flower inside.

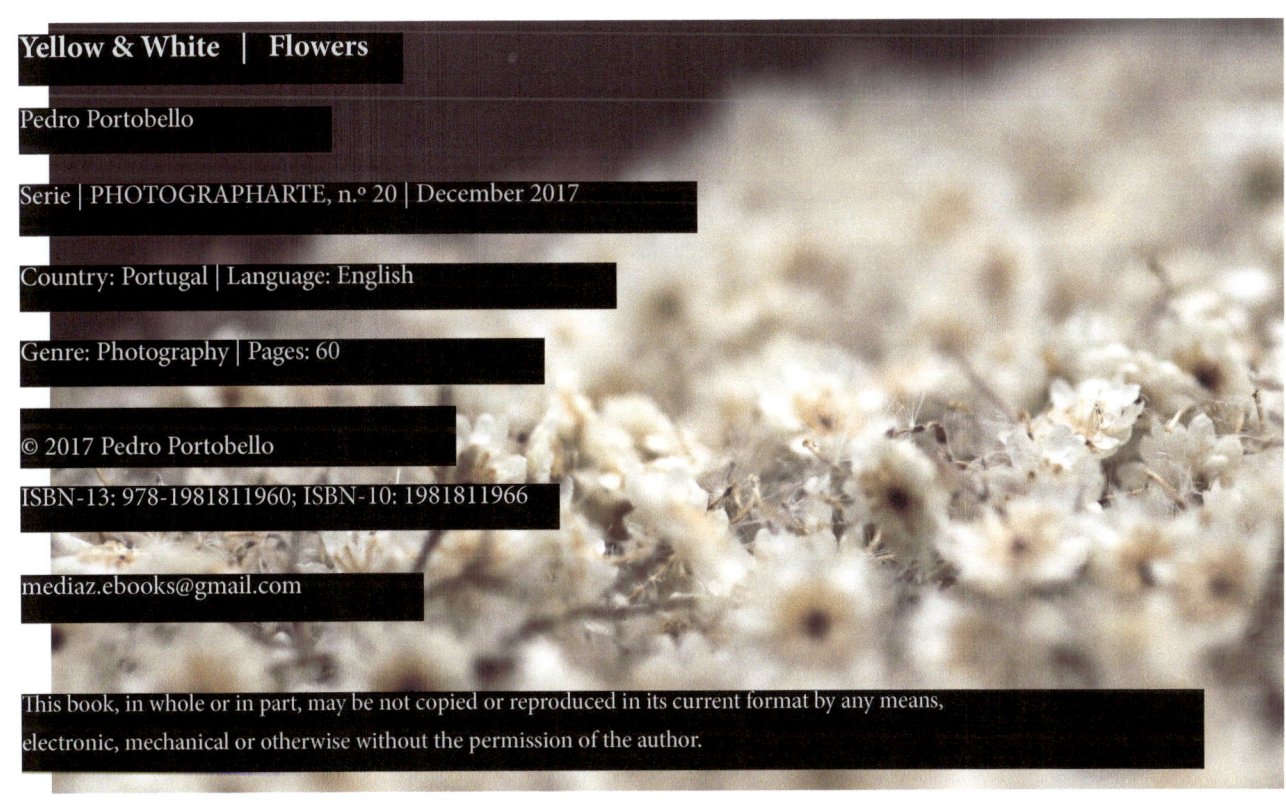

Yellow & White | Flowers

Pedro Portobello

Serie | PHOTOGRAPHARTE, n.º 20 | December 2017

Country: Portugal | Language: English

Genre: Photography | Pages: 60

© 2017 Pedro Portobello

ISBN-13: 978-1981811960; ISBN-10: 1981811966

mediaz.ebooks@gmail.com

This book, in whole or in part, may be not copied or reproduced in its current format by any means, electronic, mechanical or otherwise without the permission of the author.

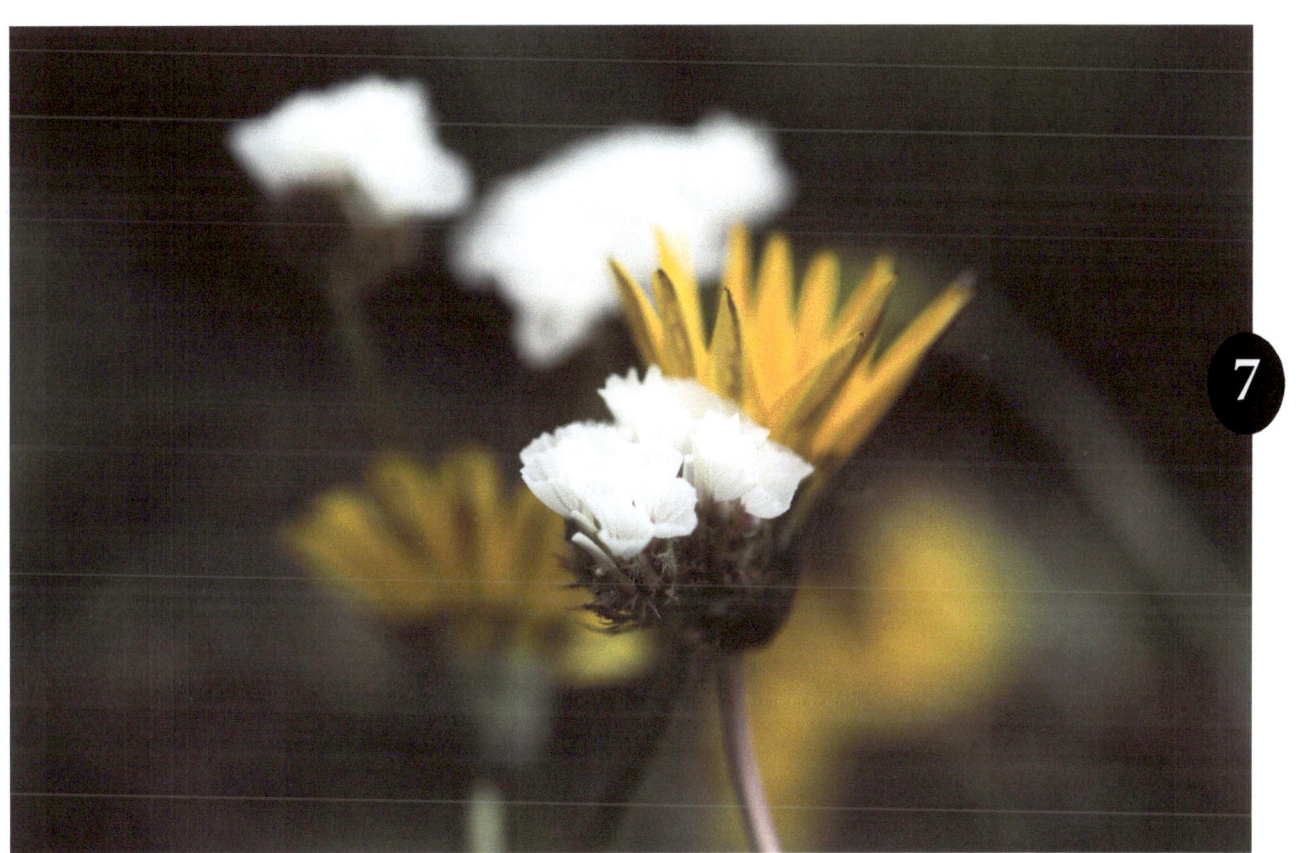

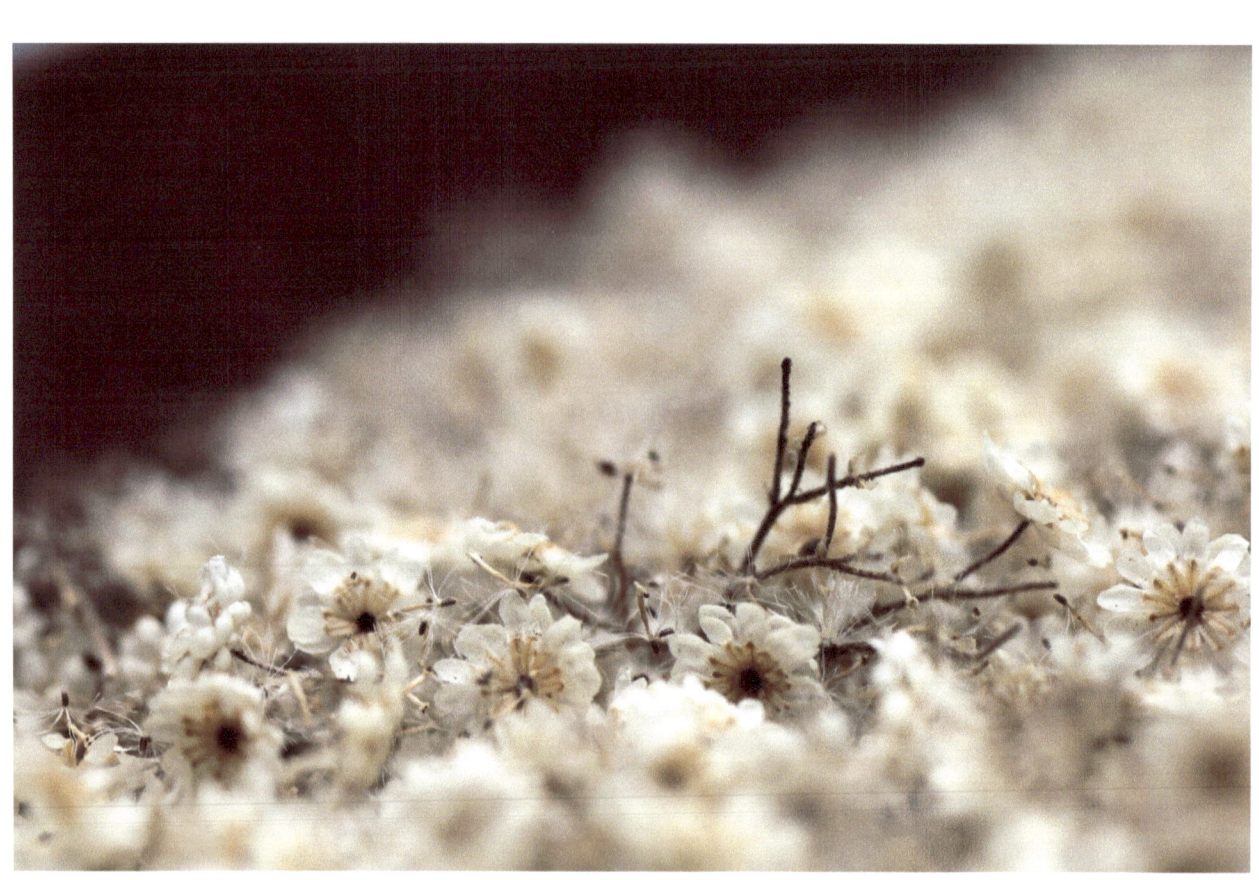

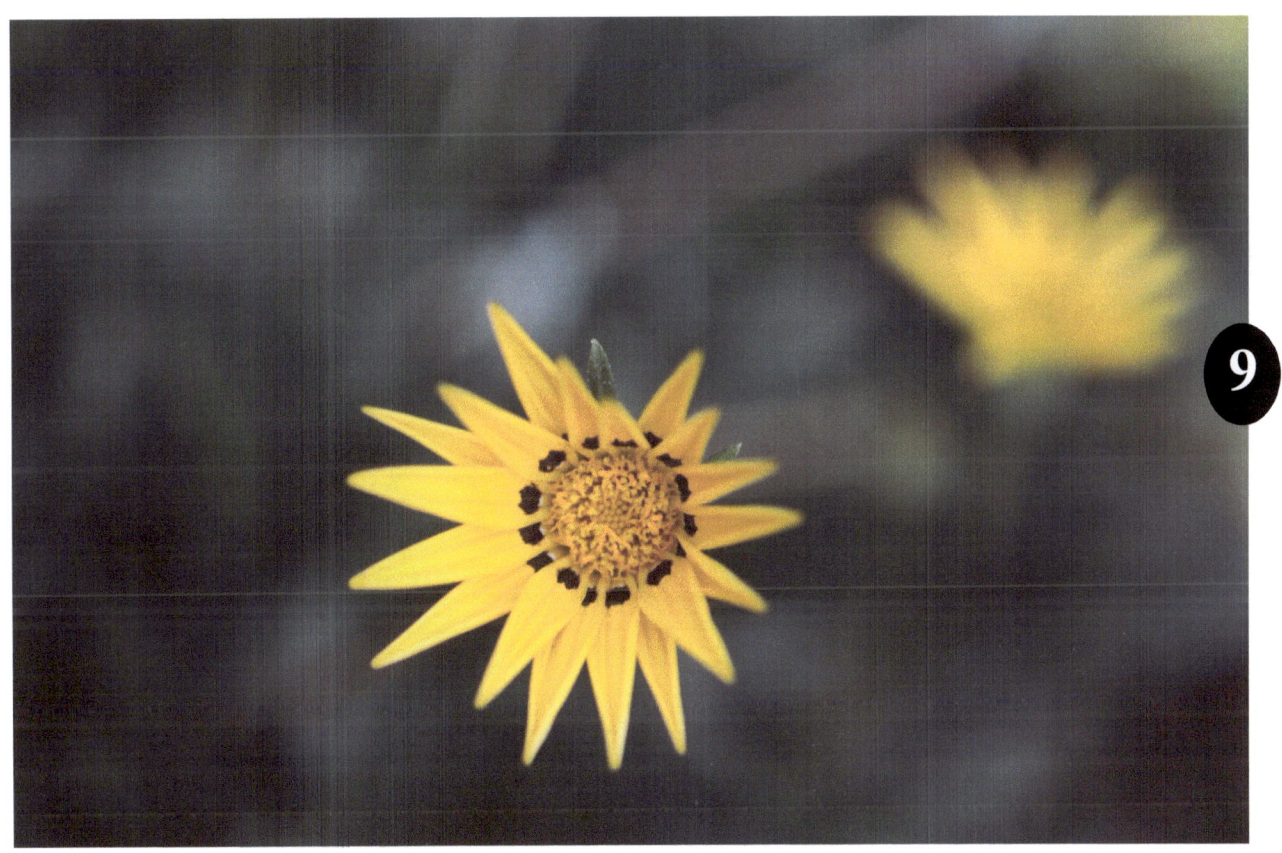

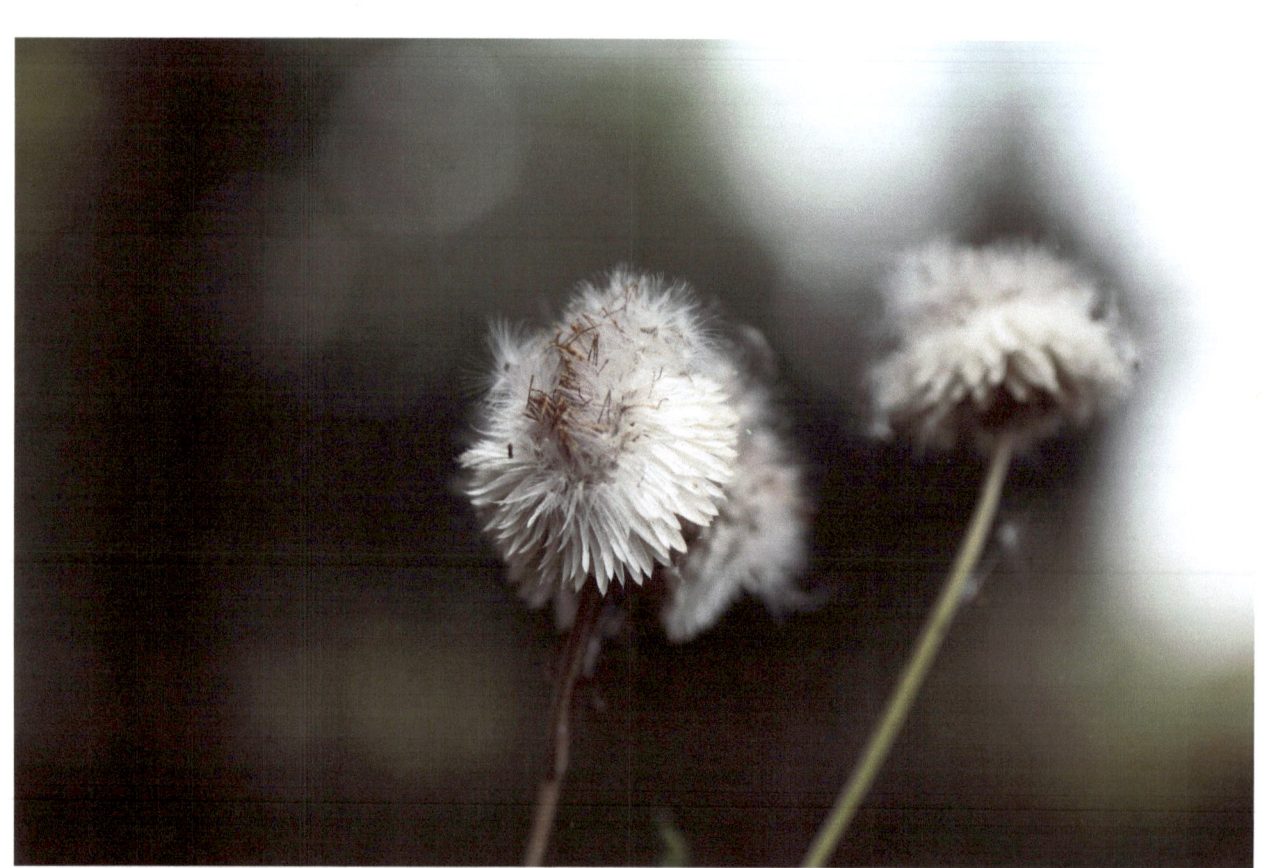

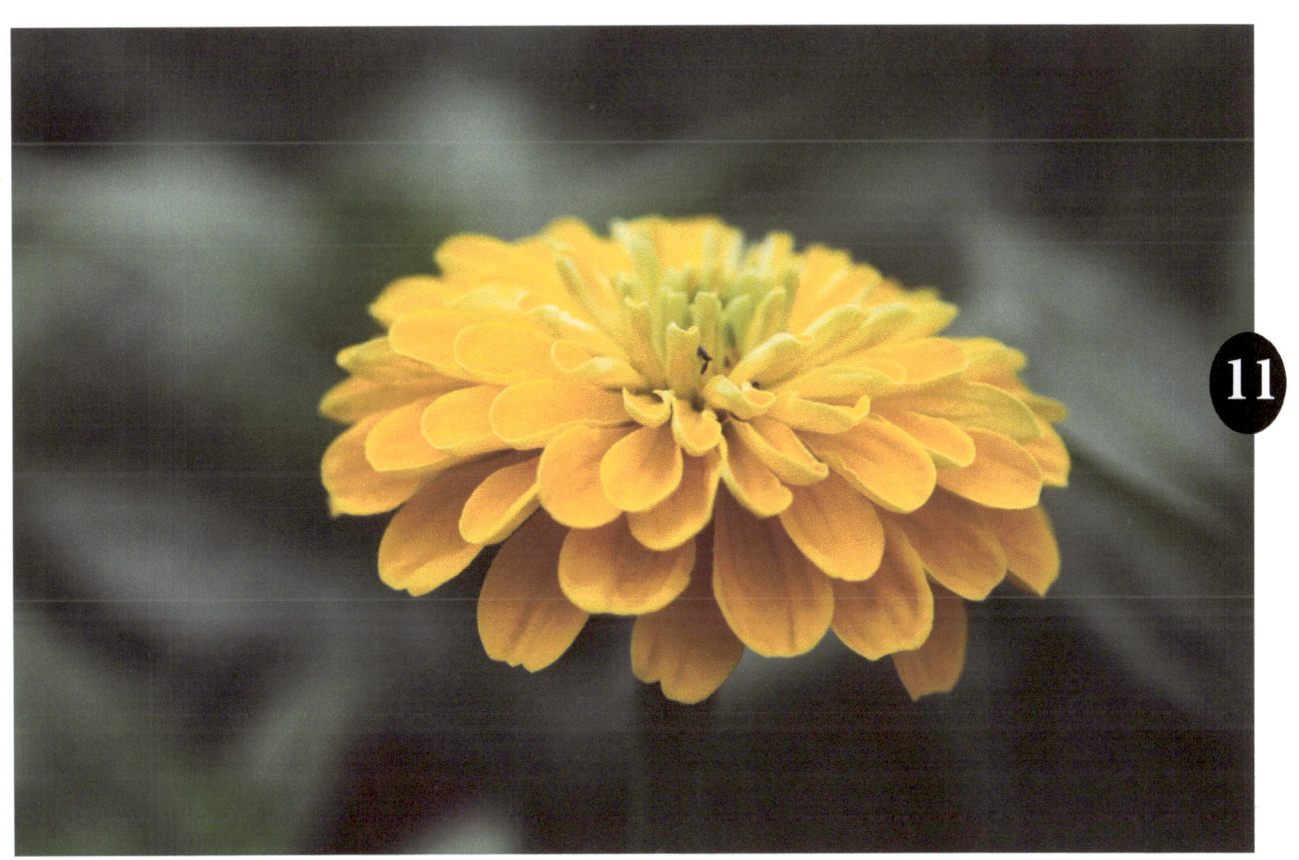

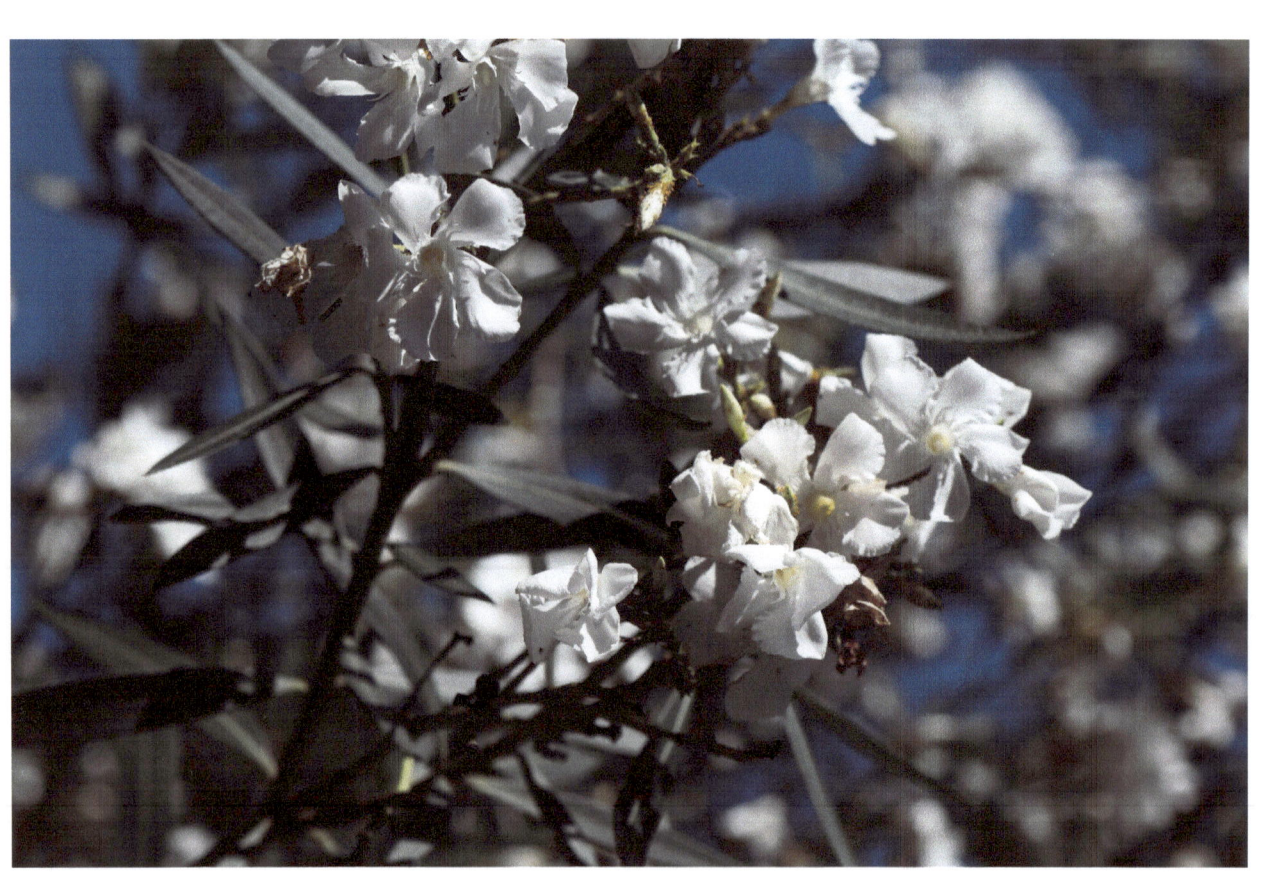

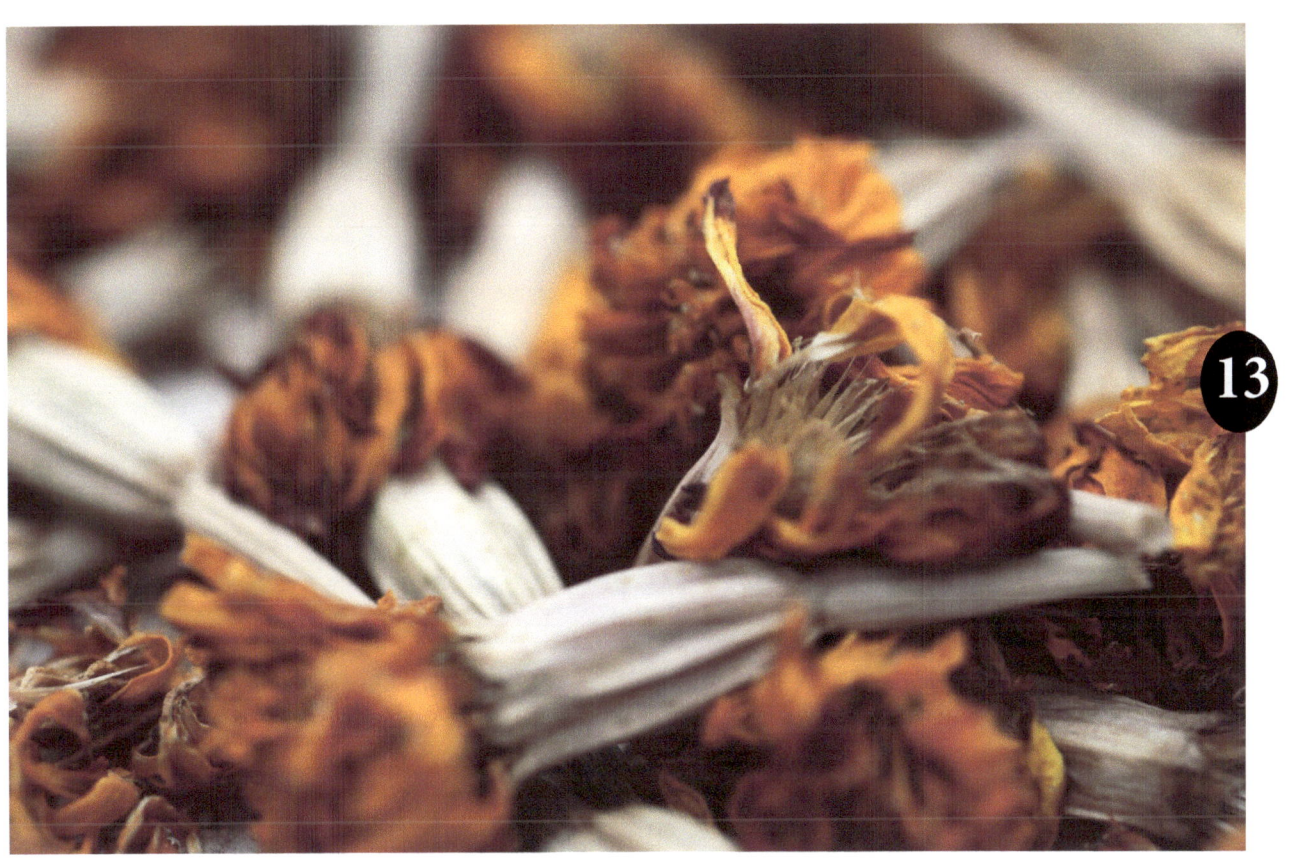

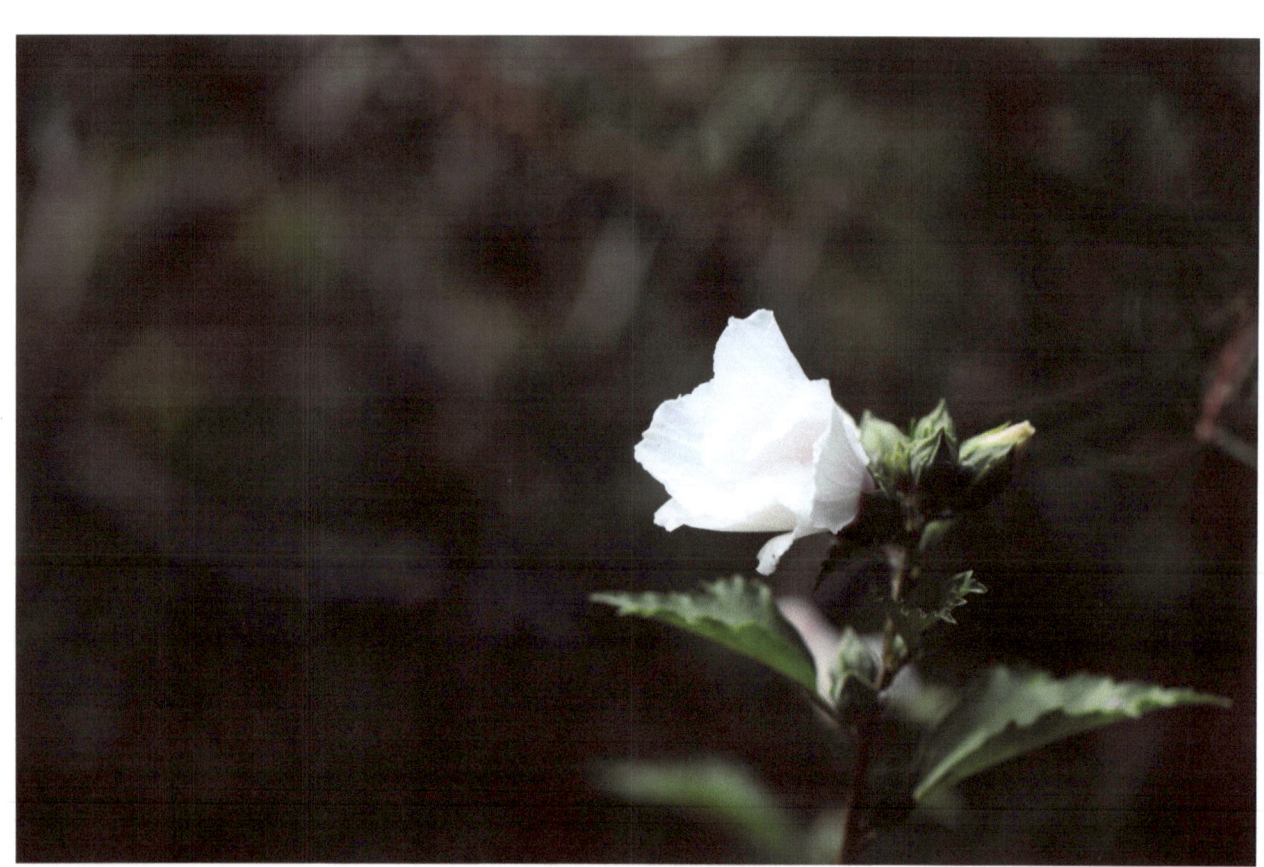

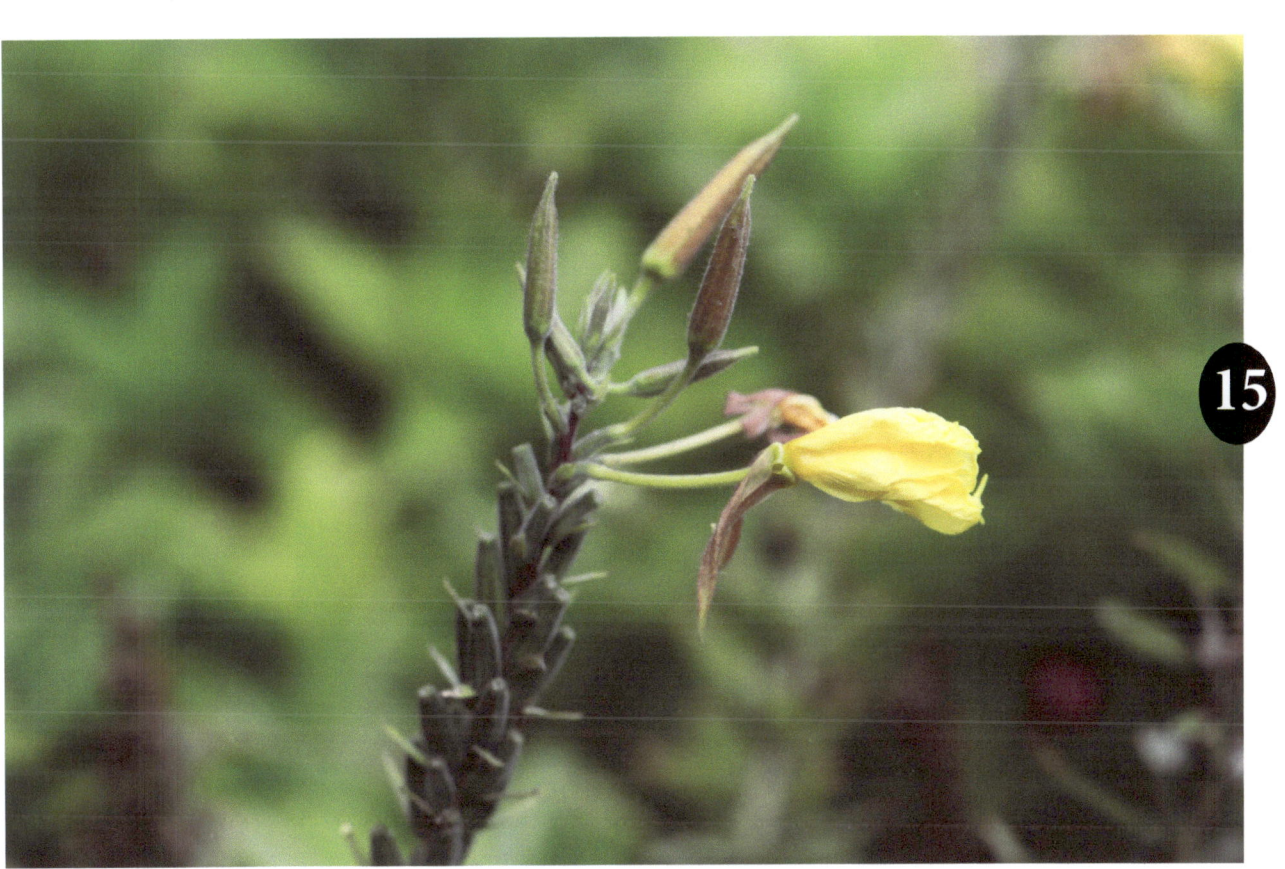

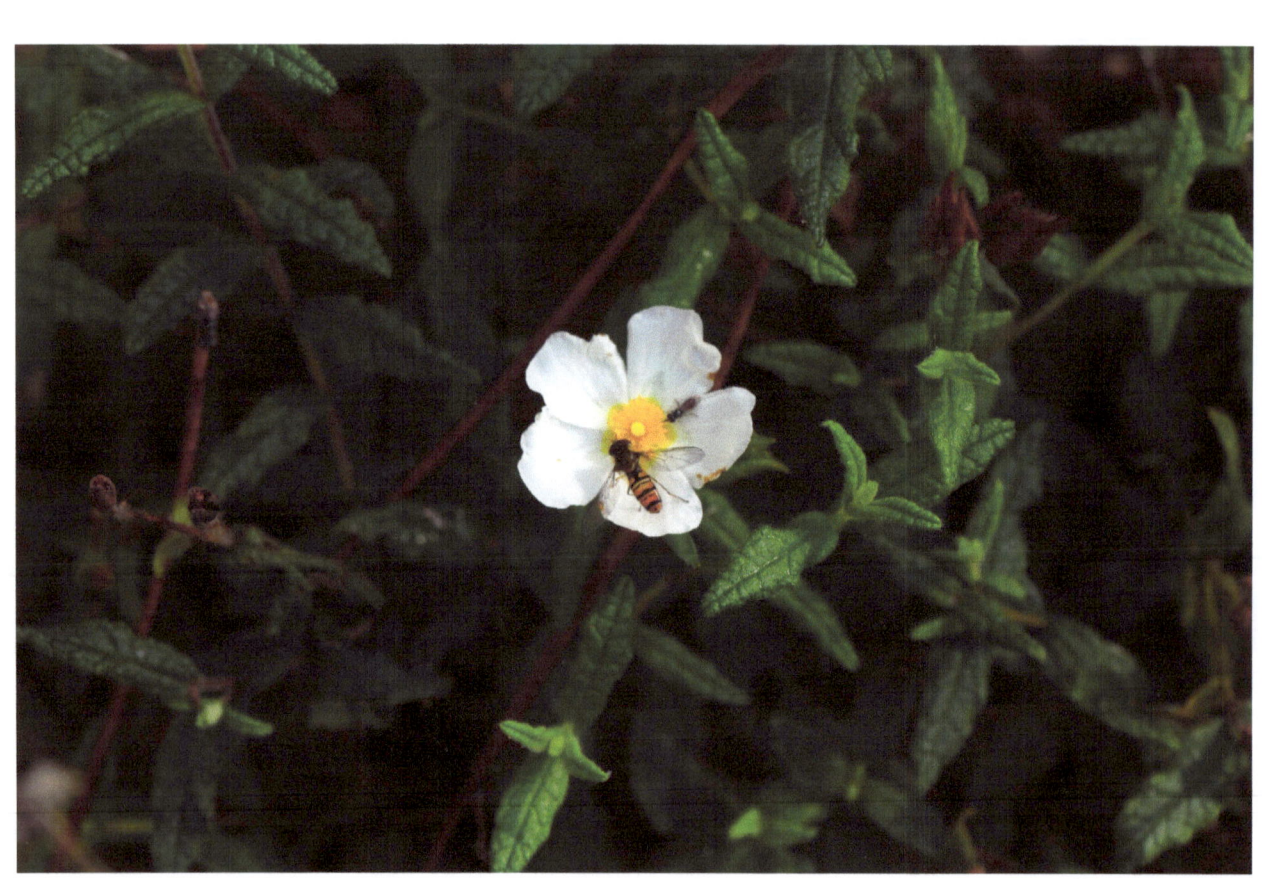

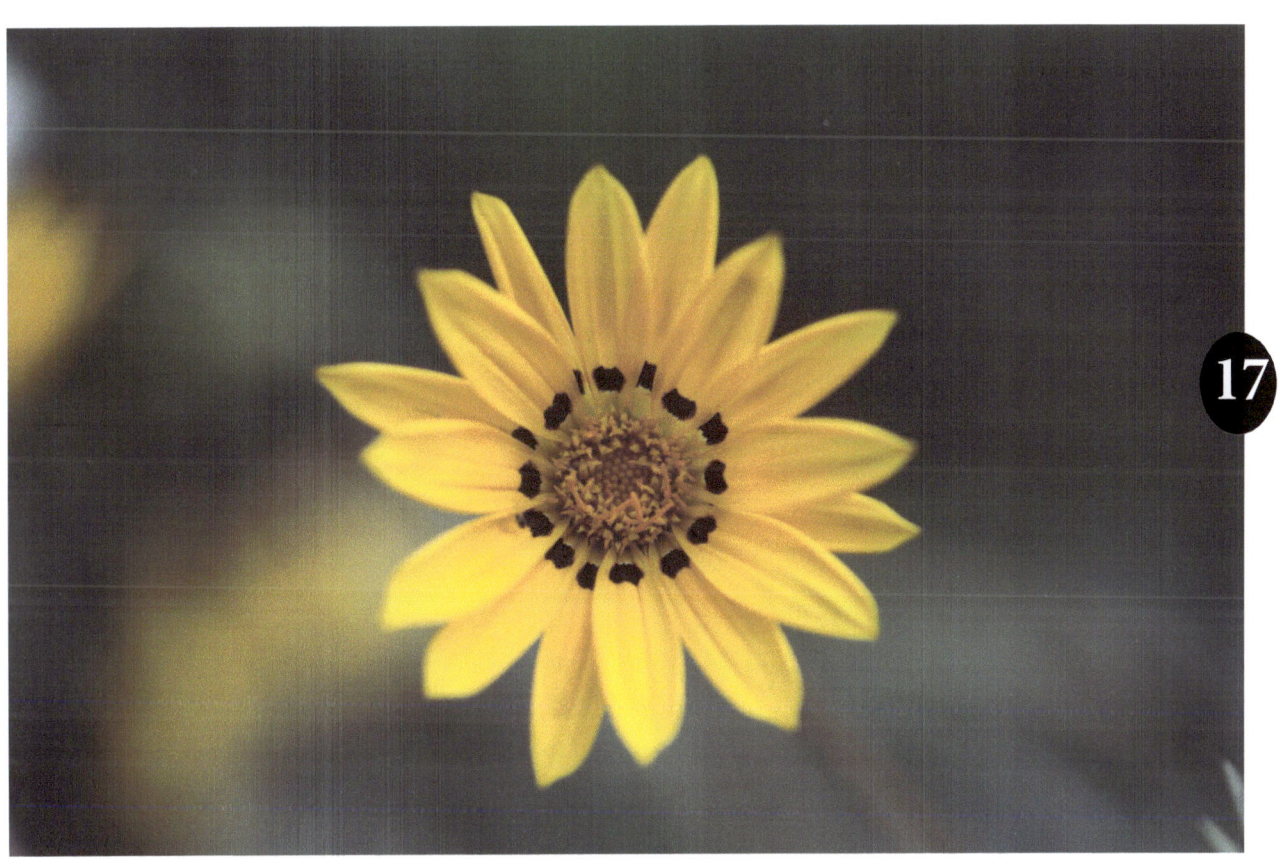

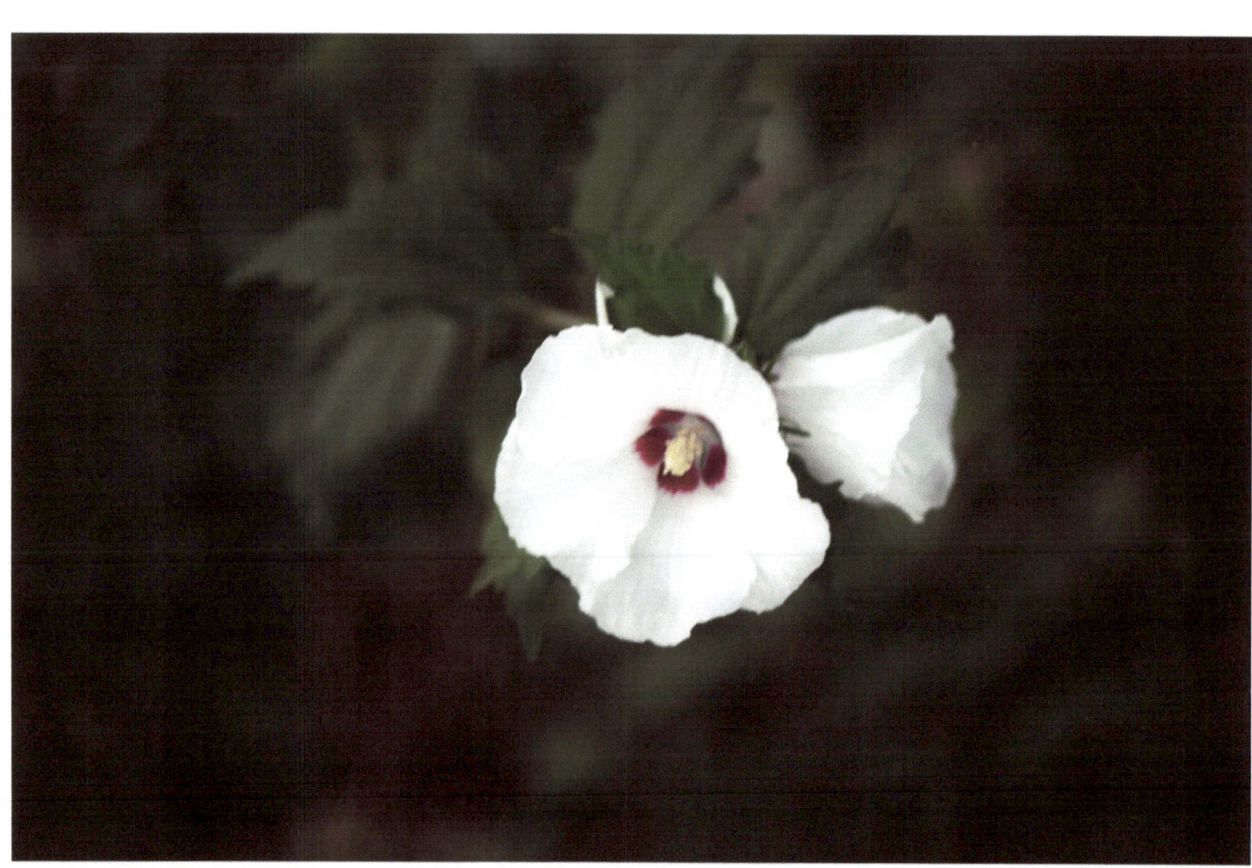

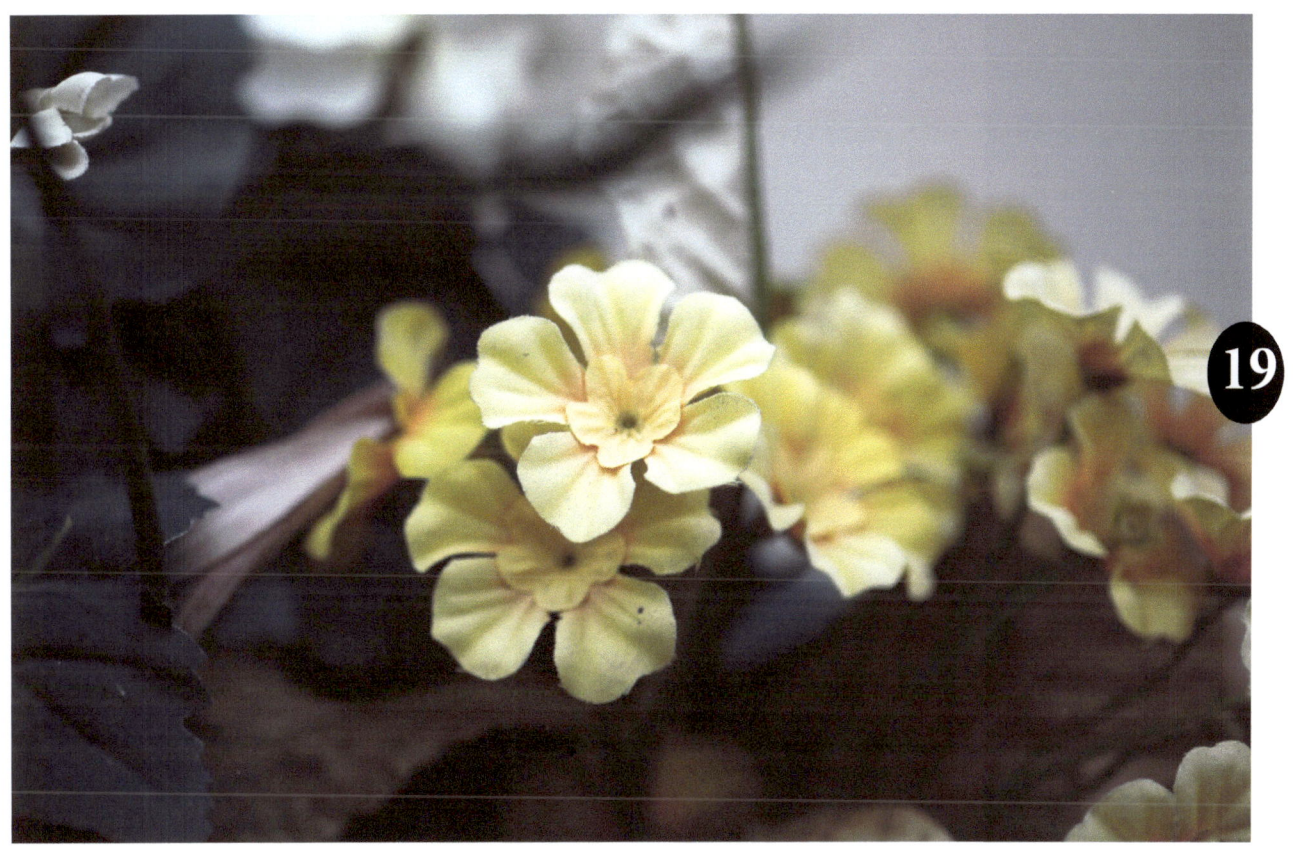

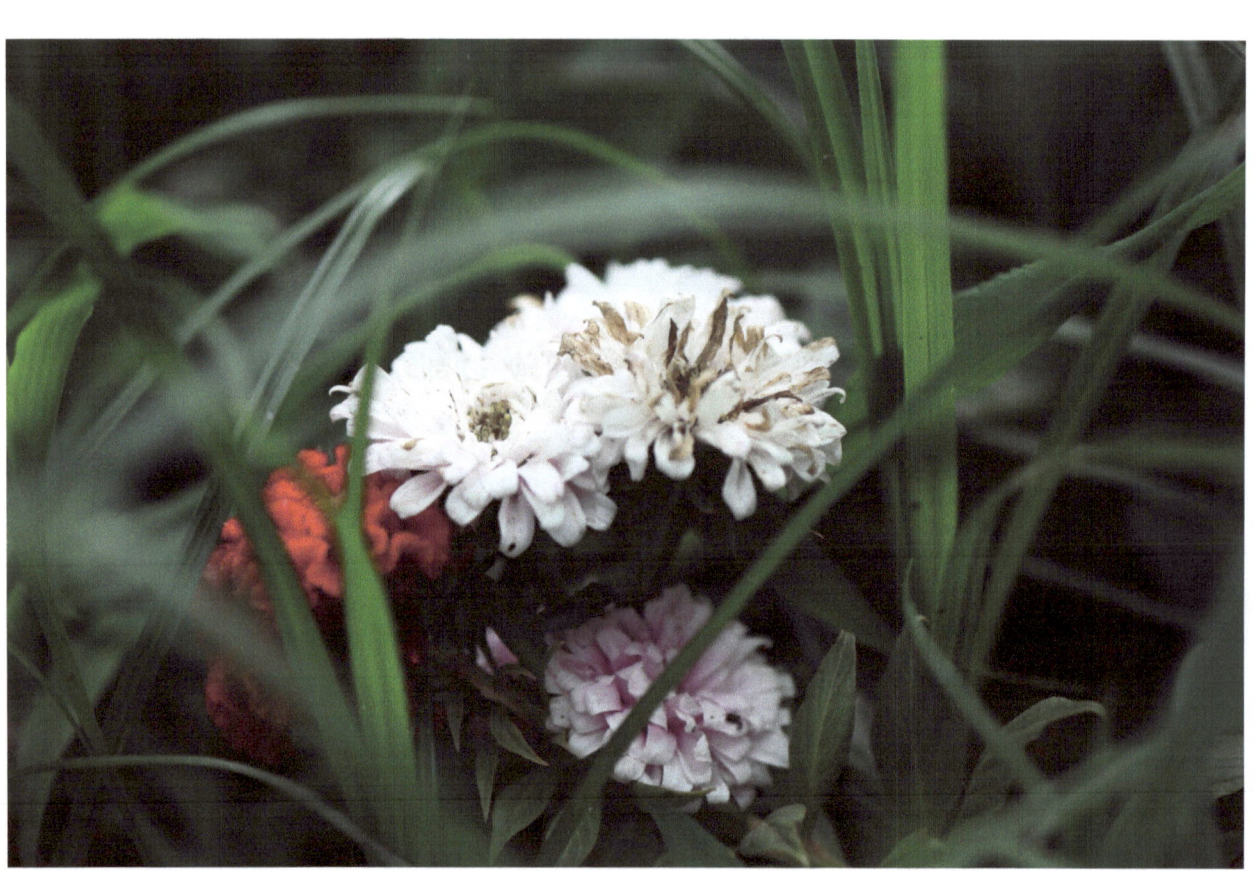

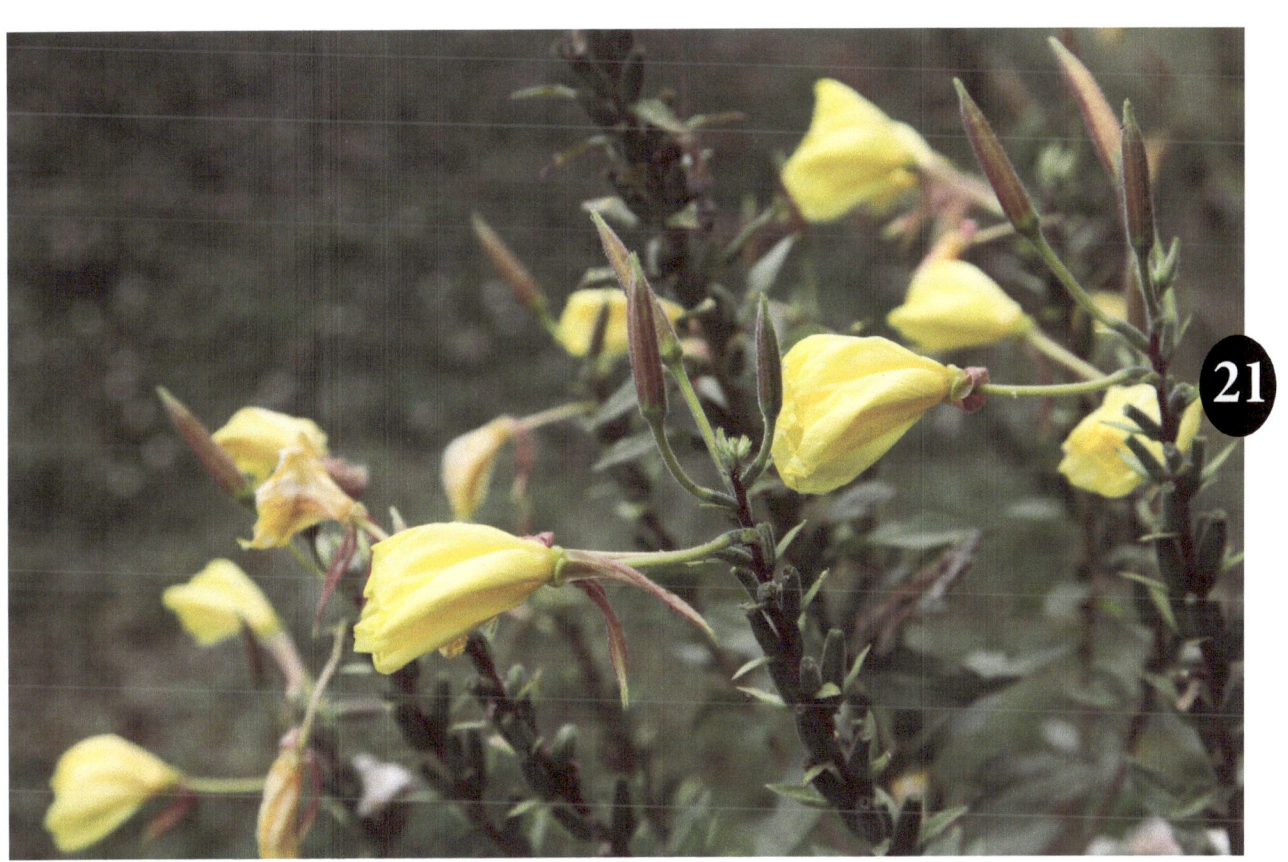

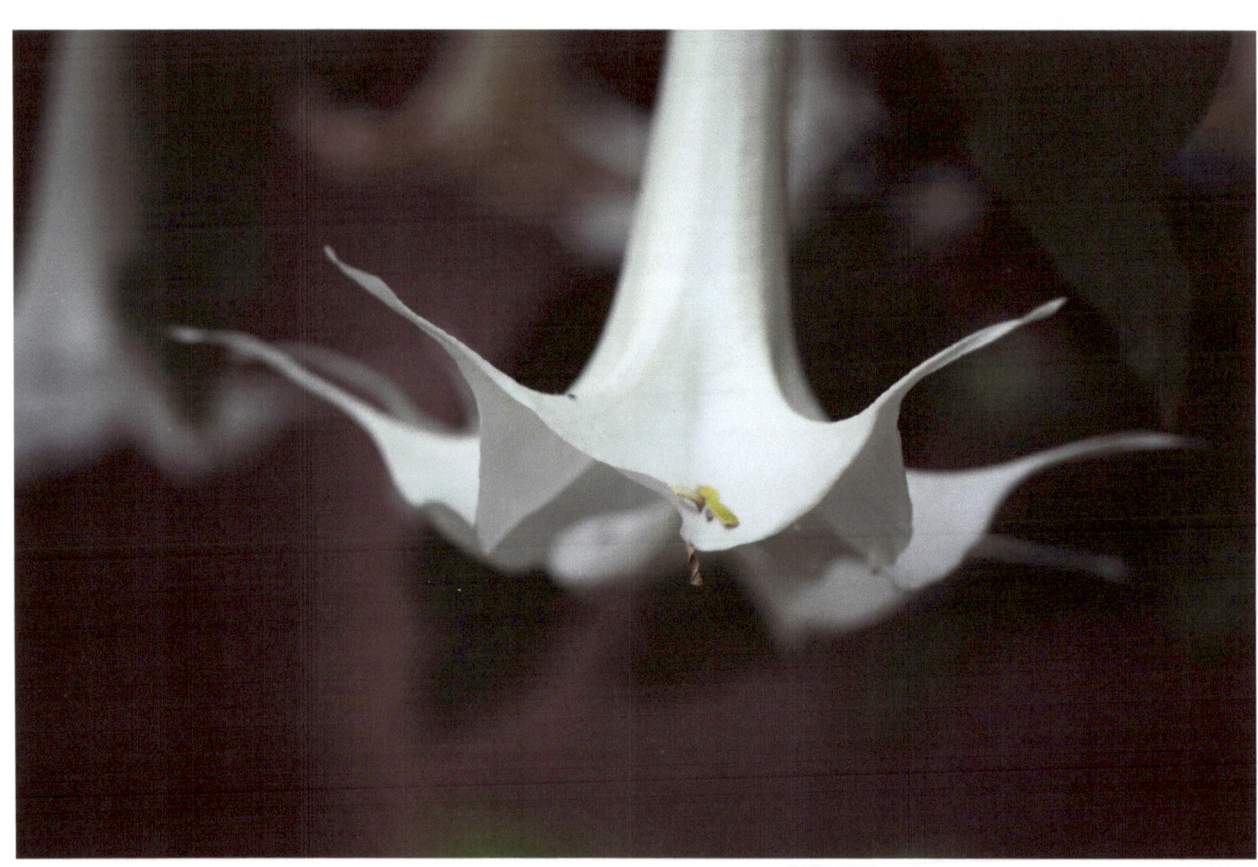

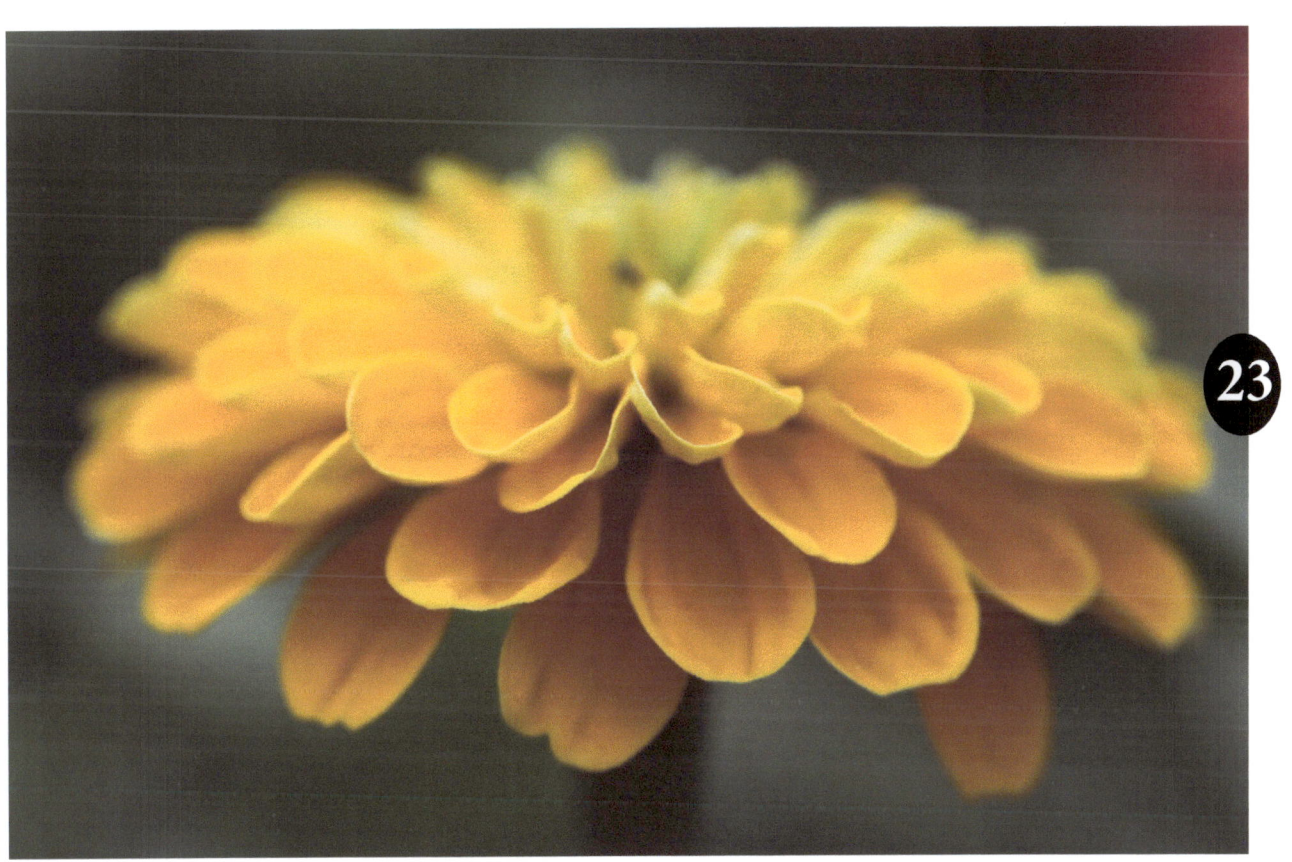

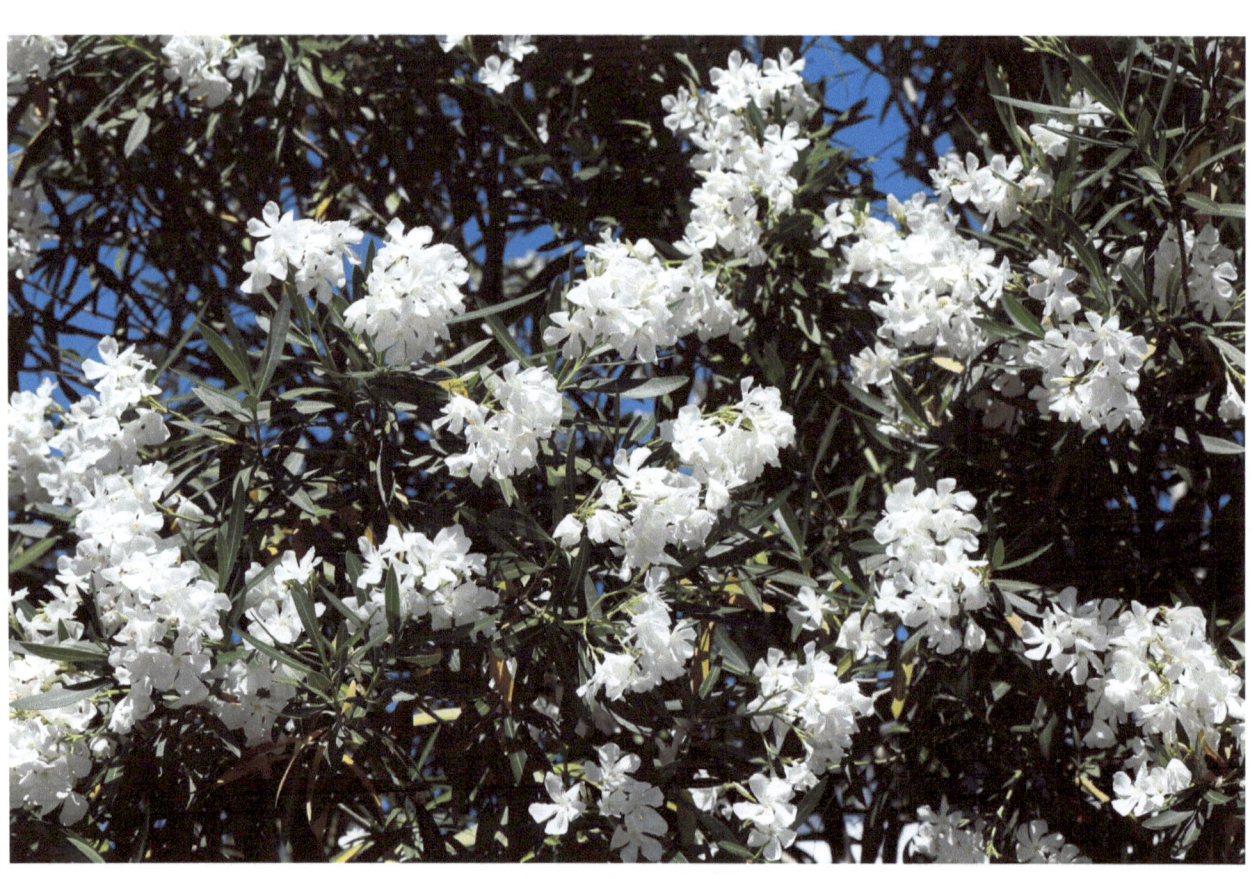

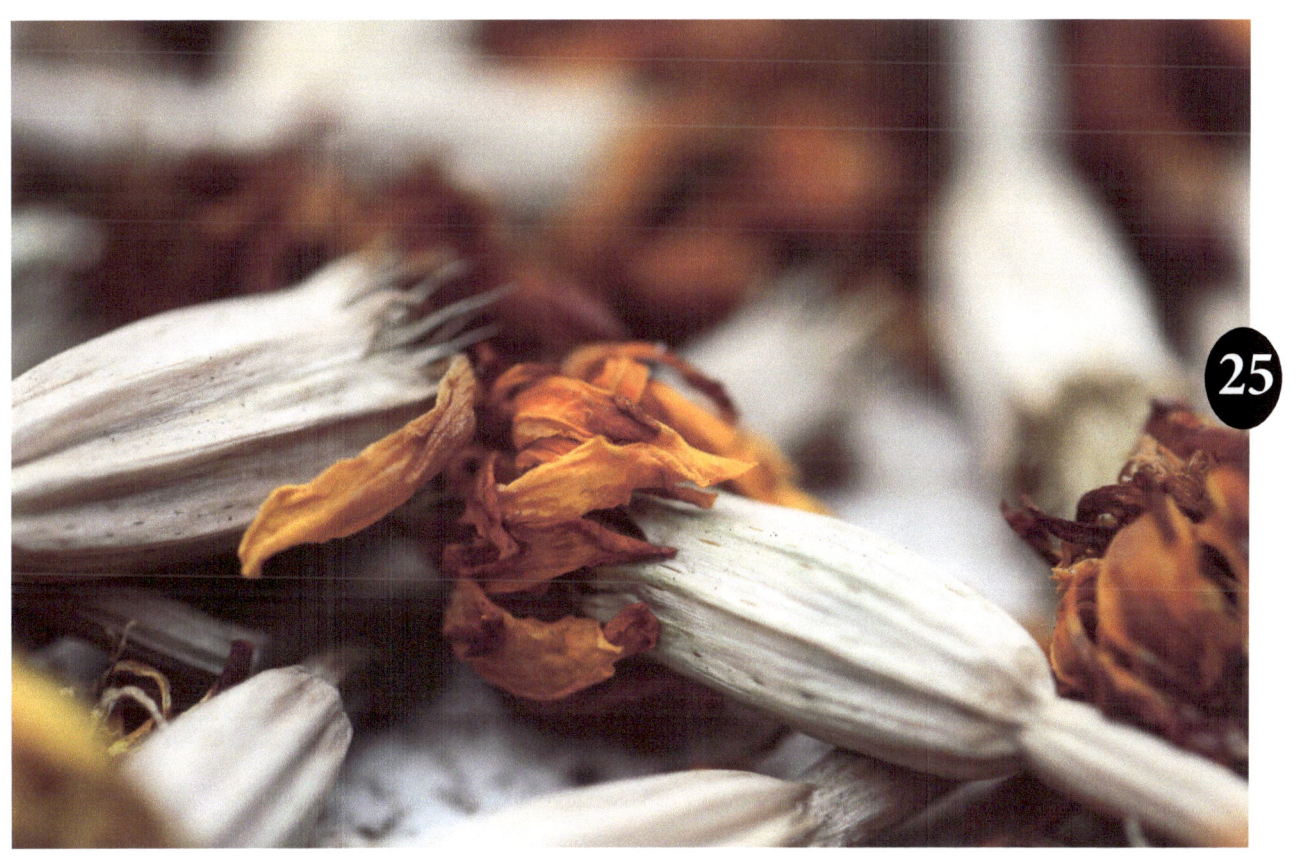

25

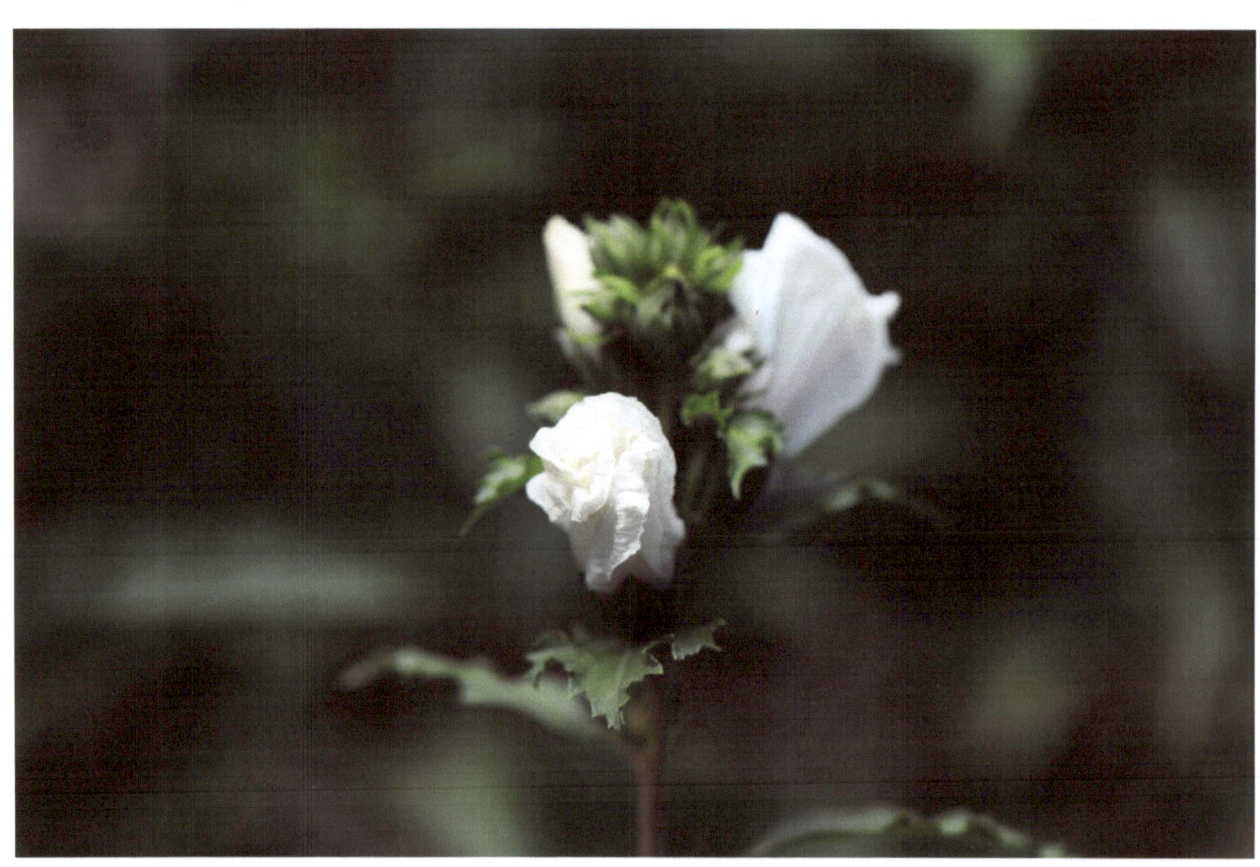

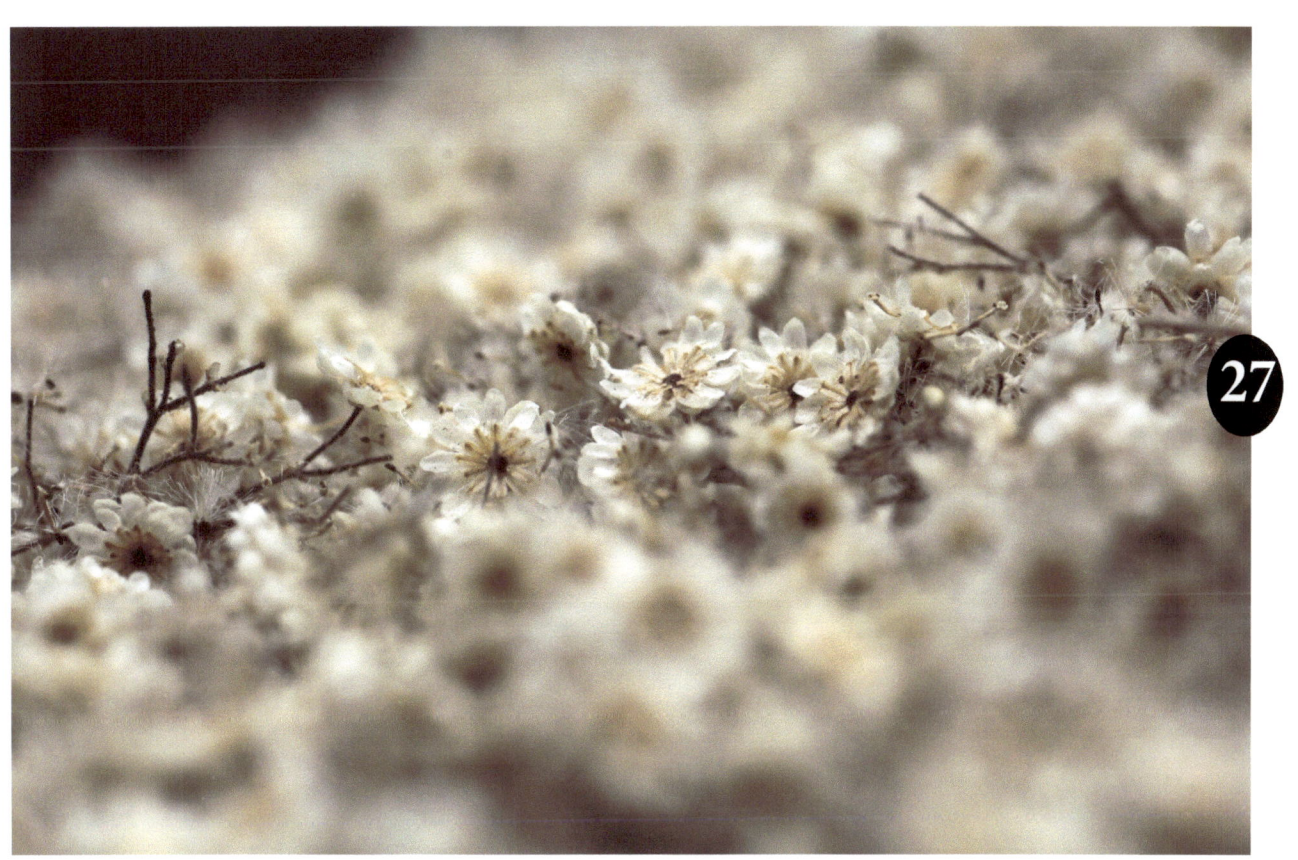

27

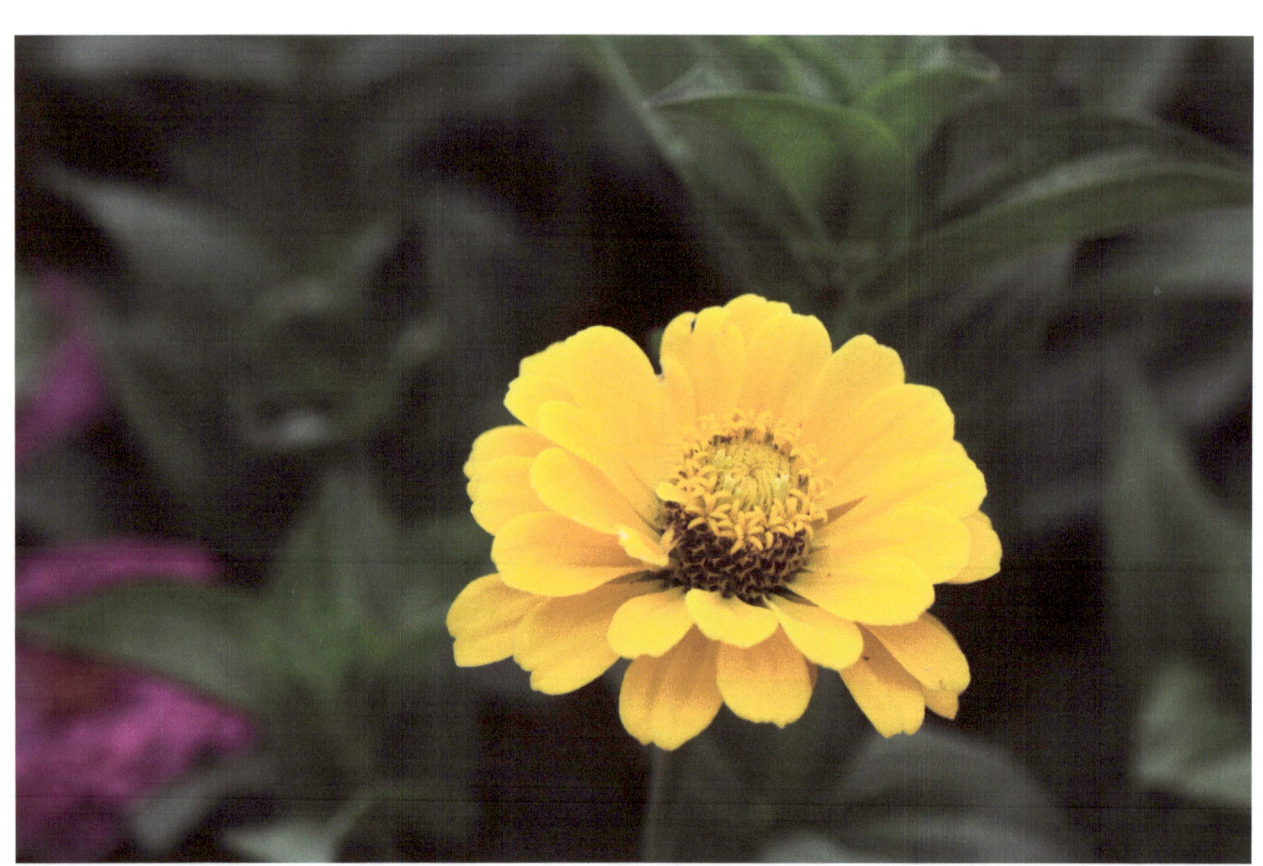

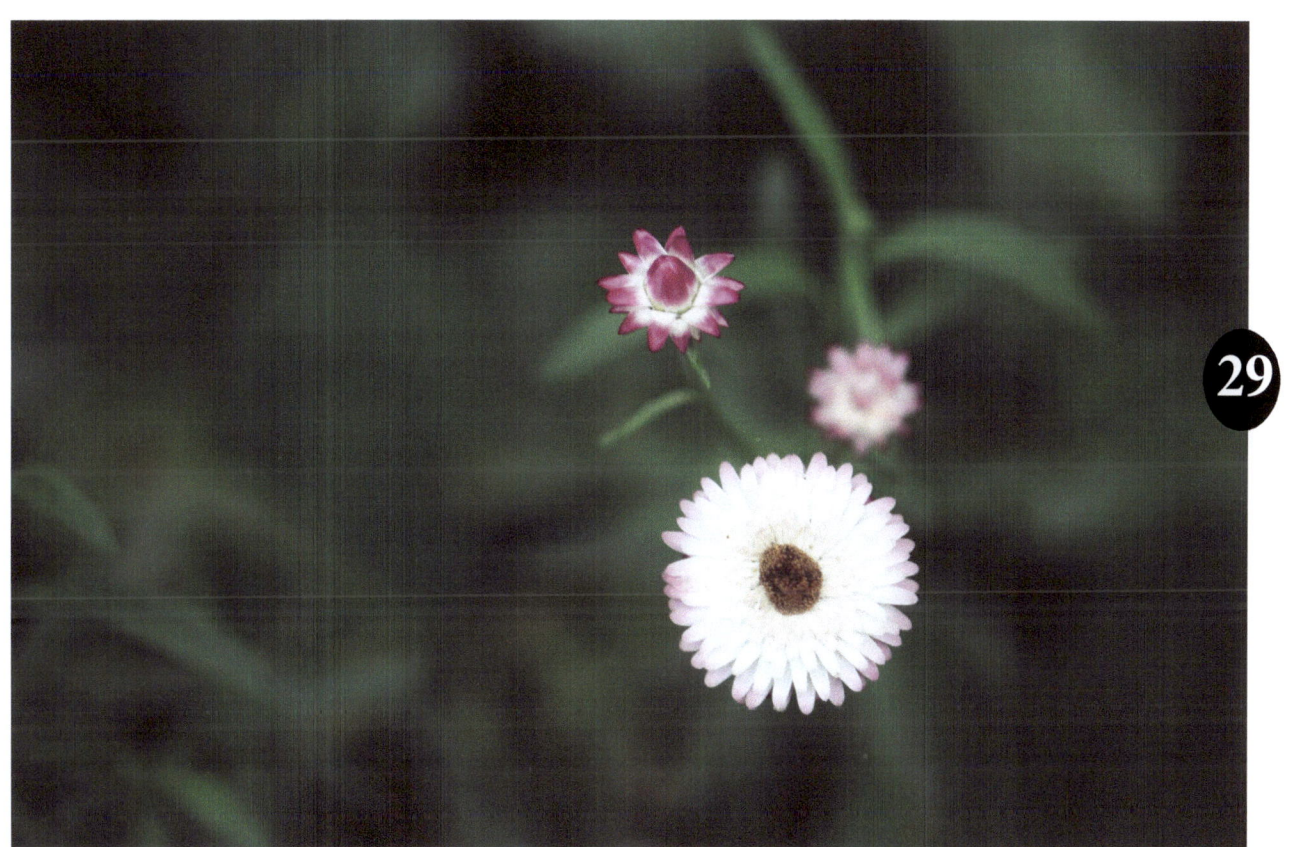

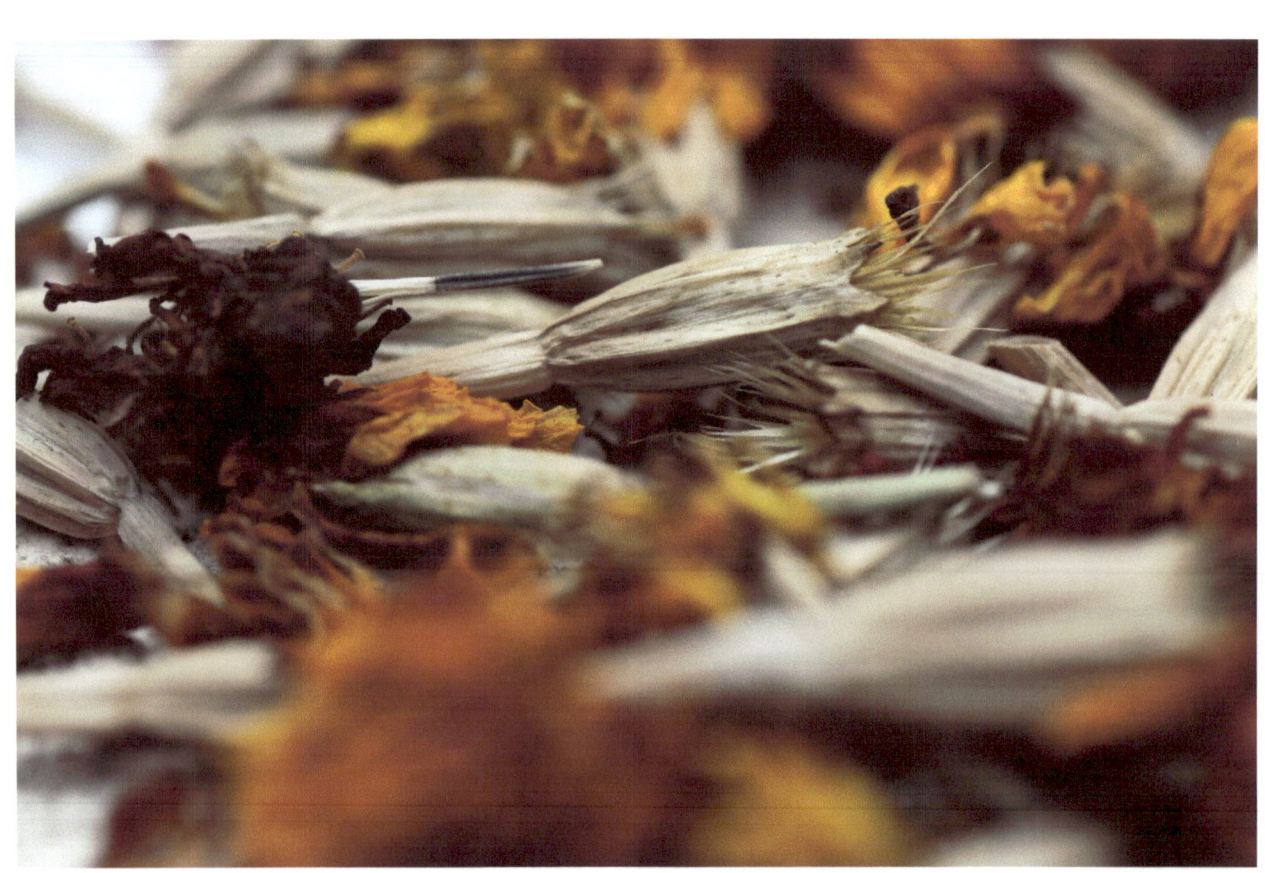

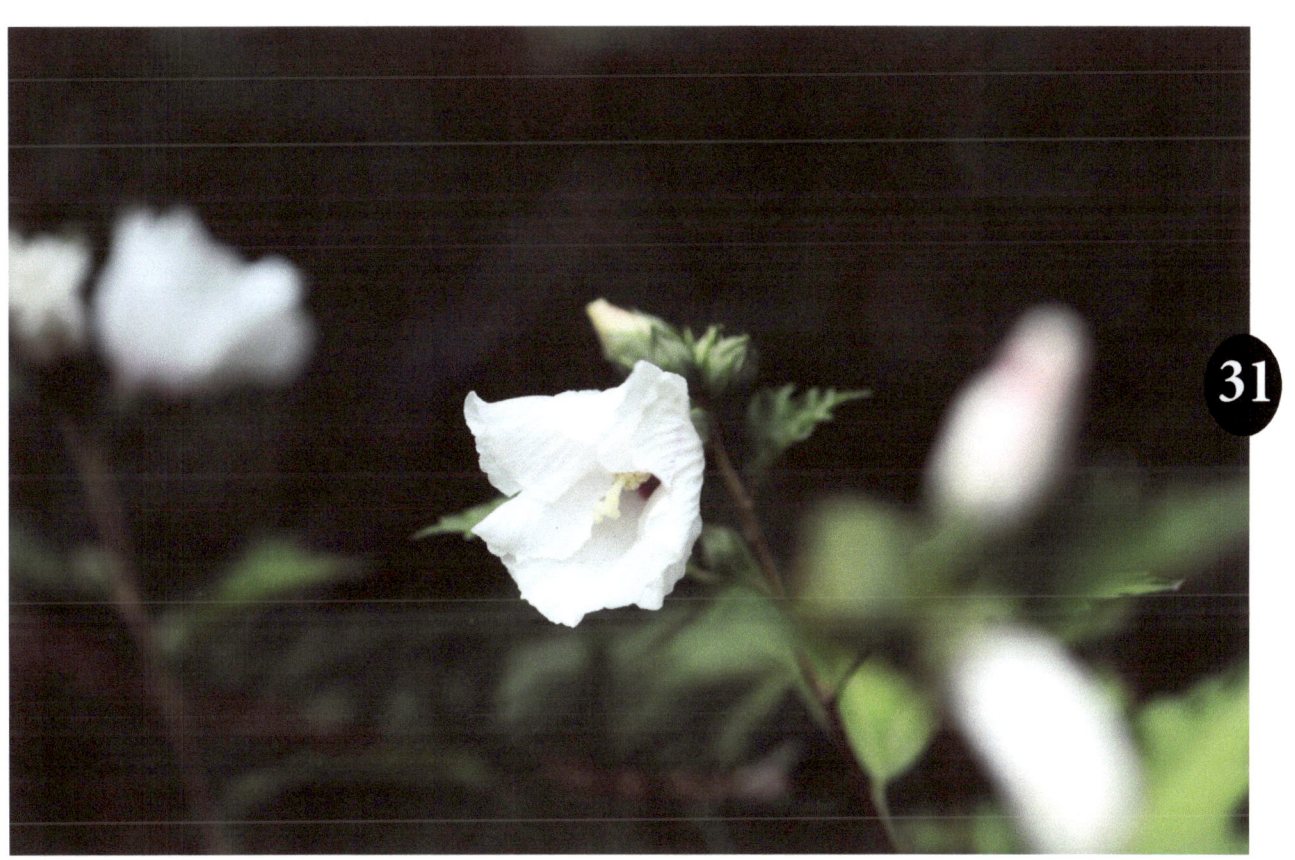

31

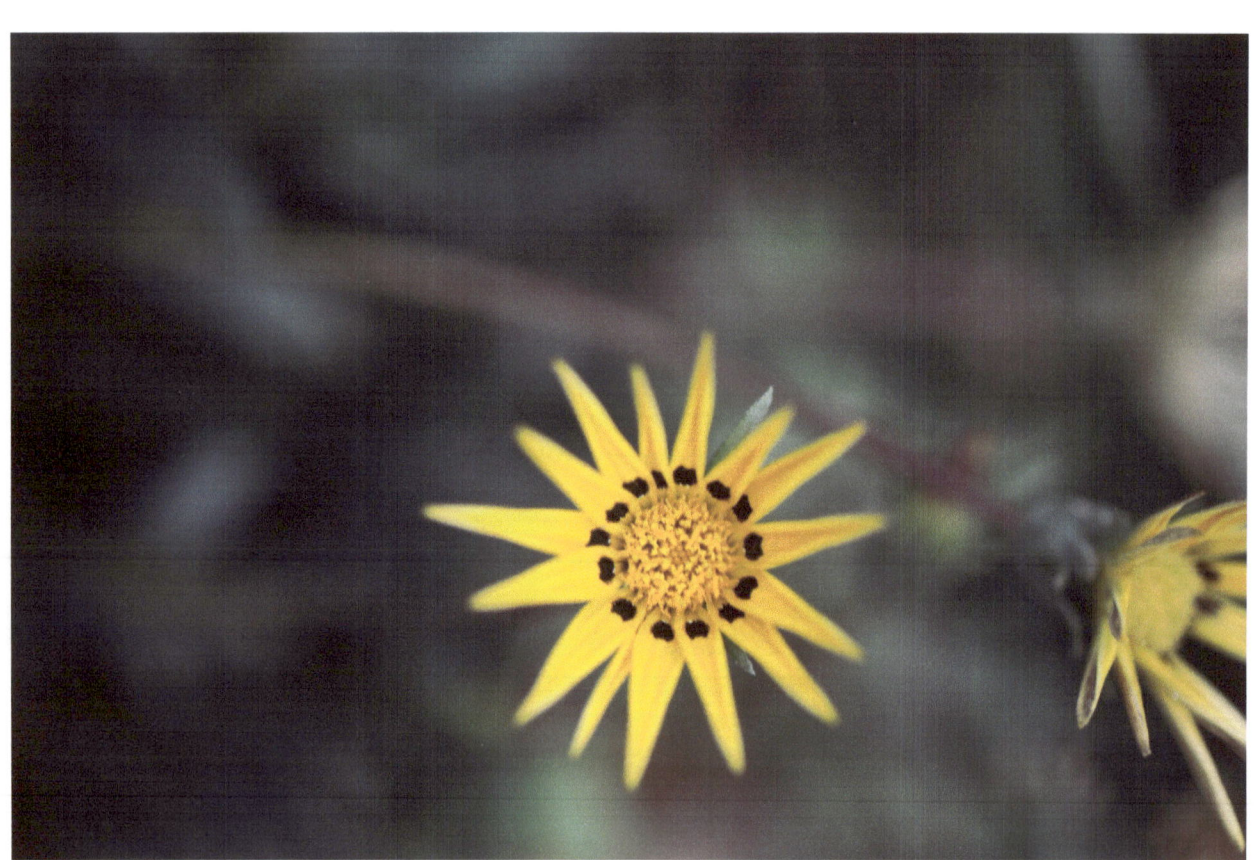

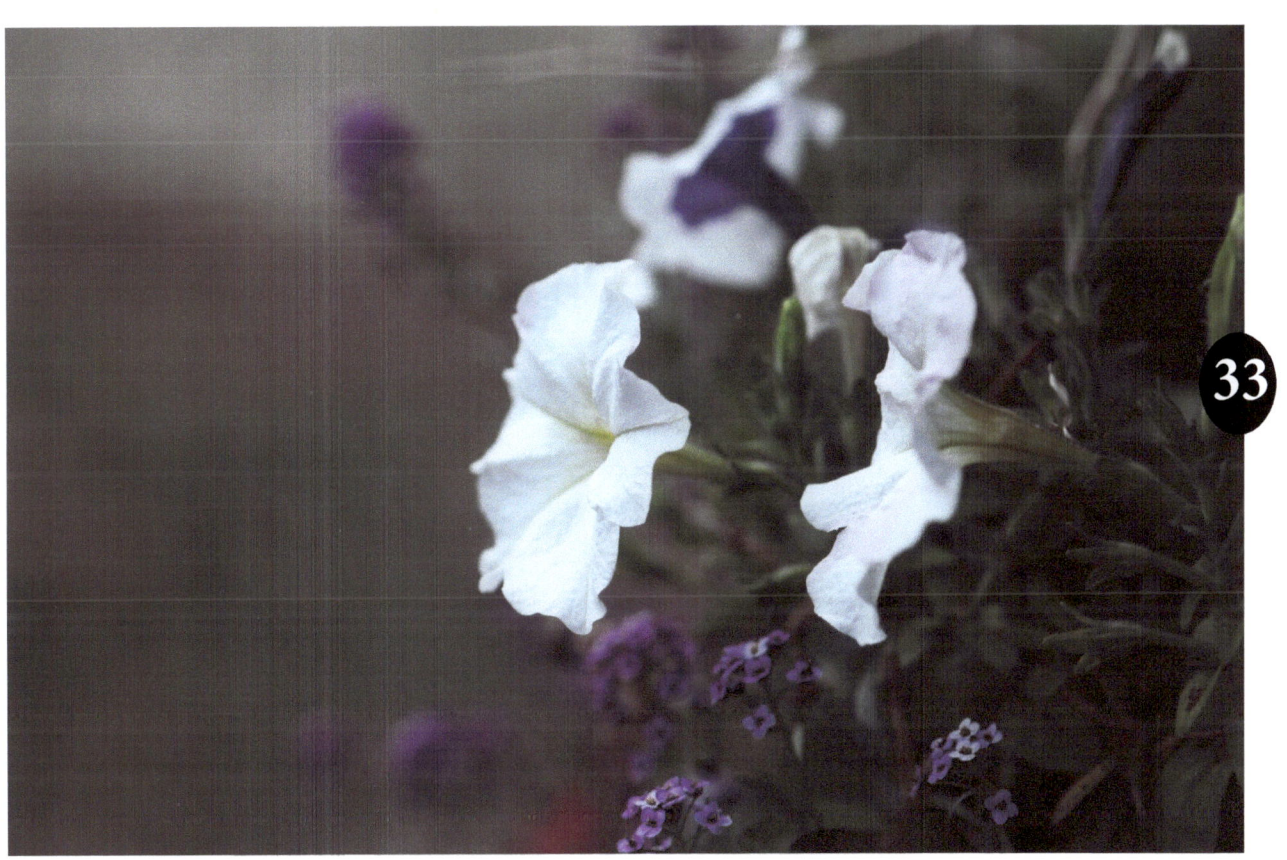

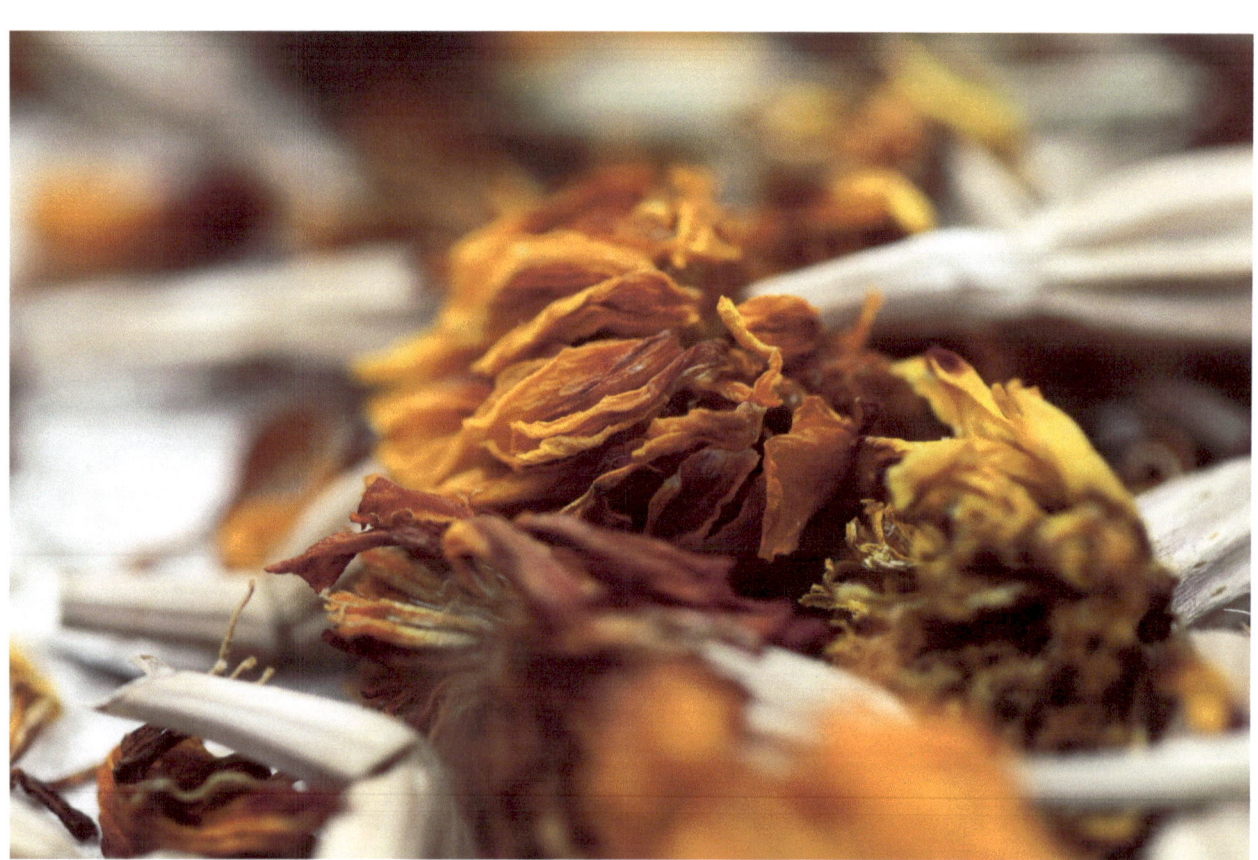

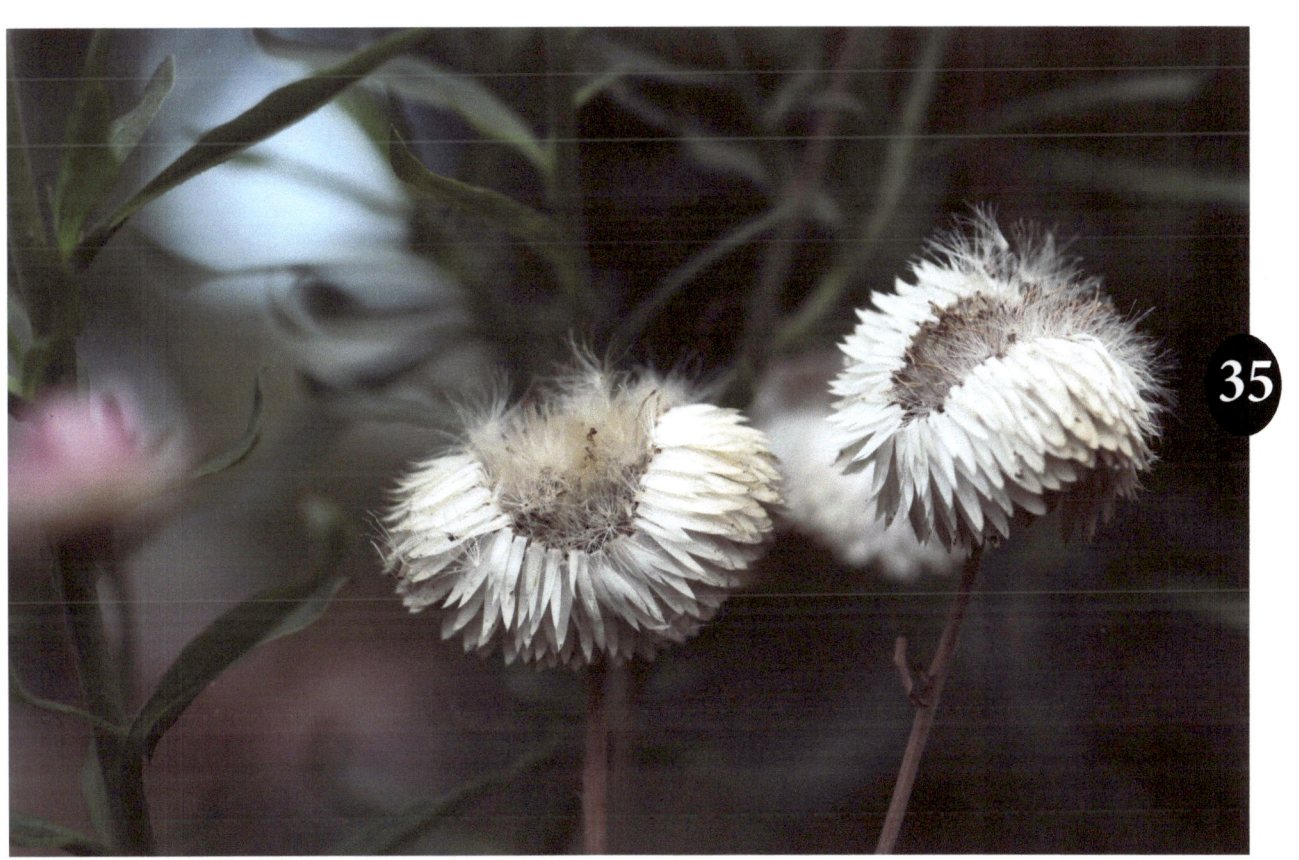

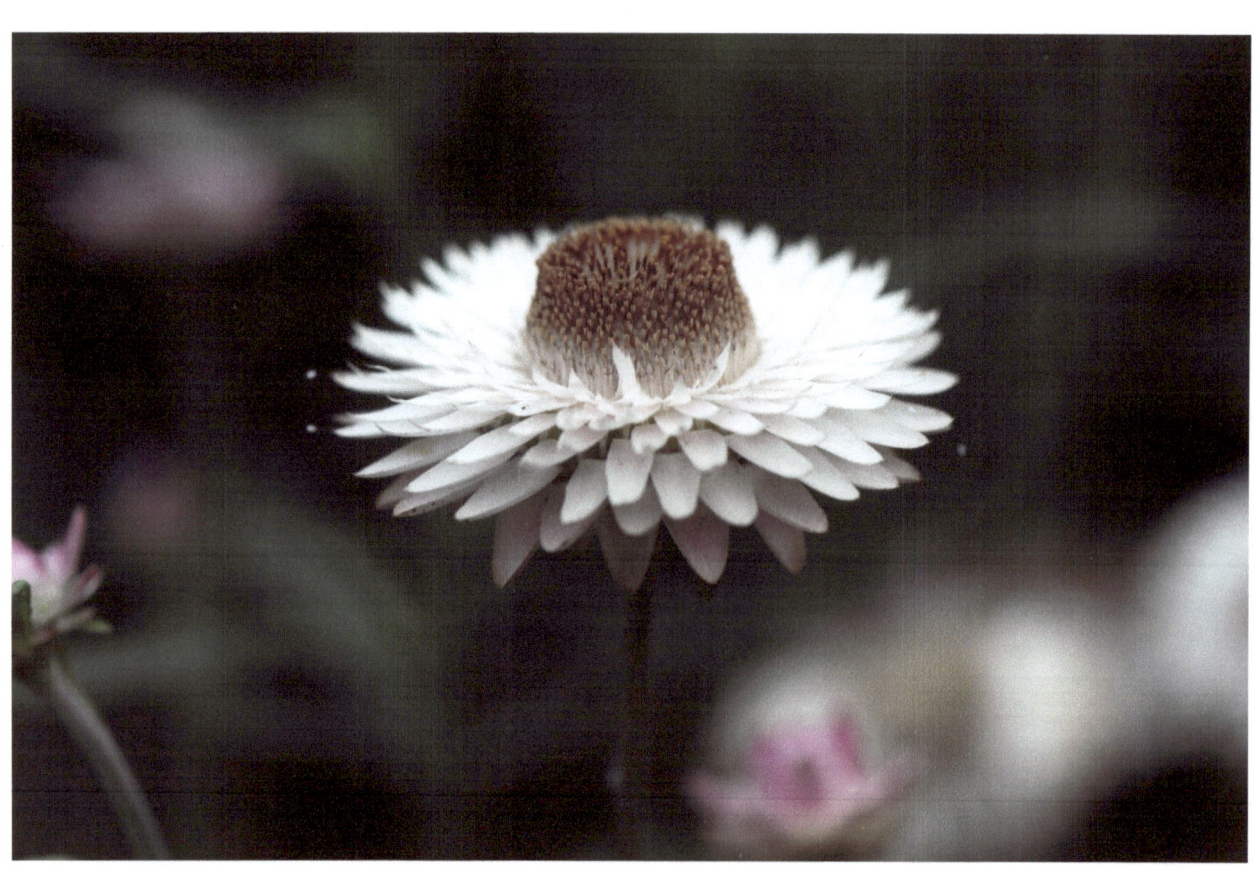

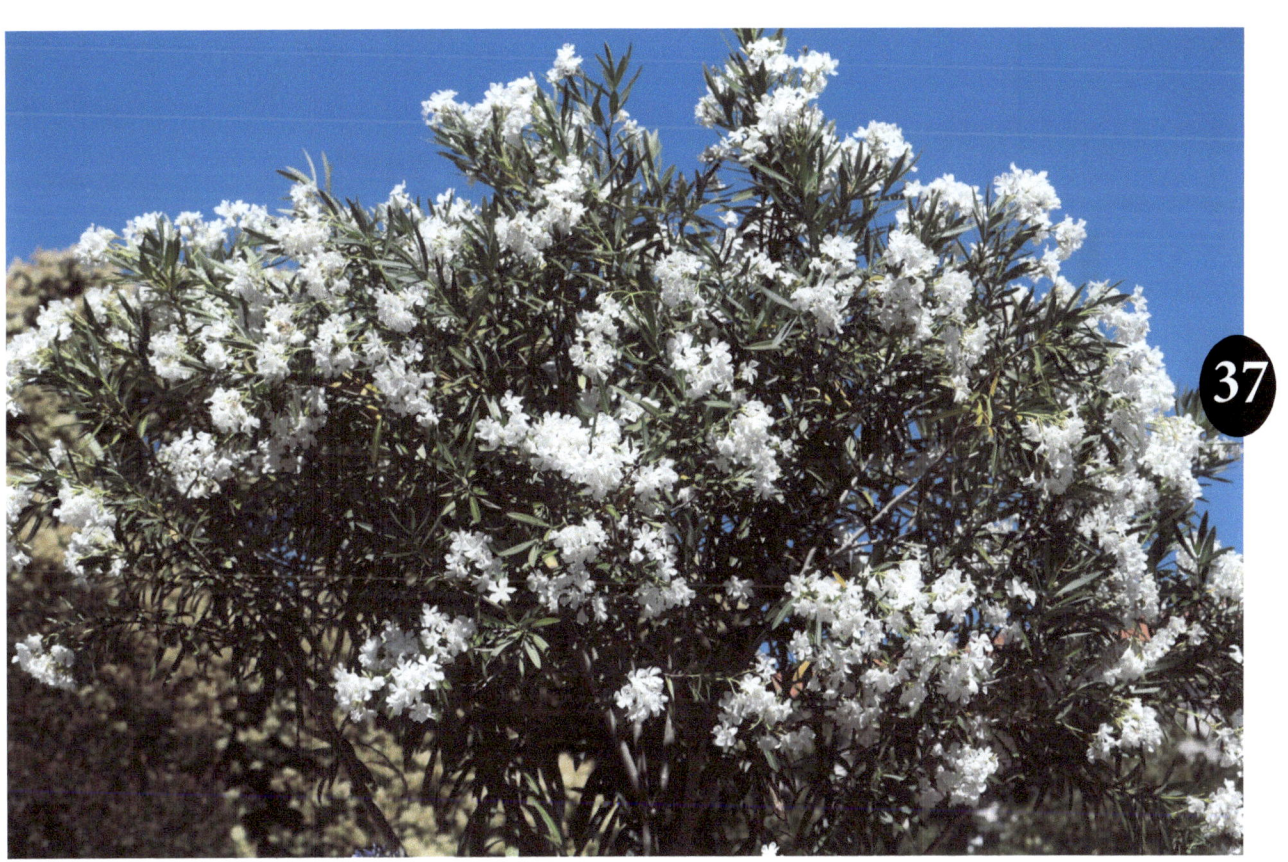

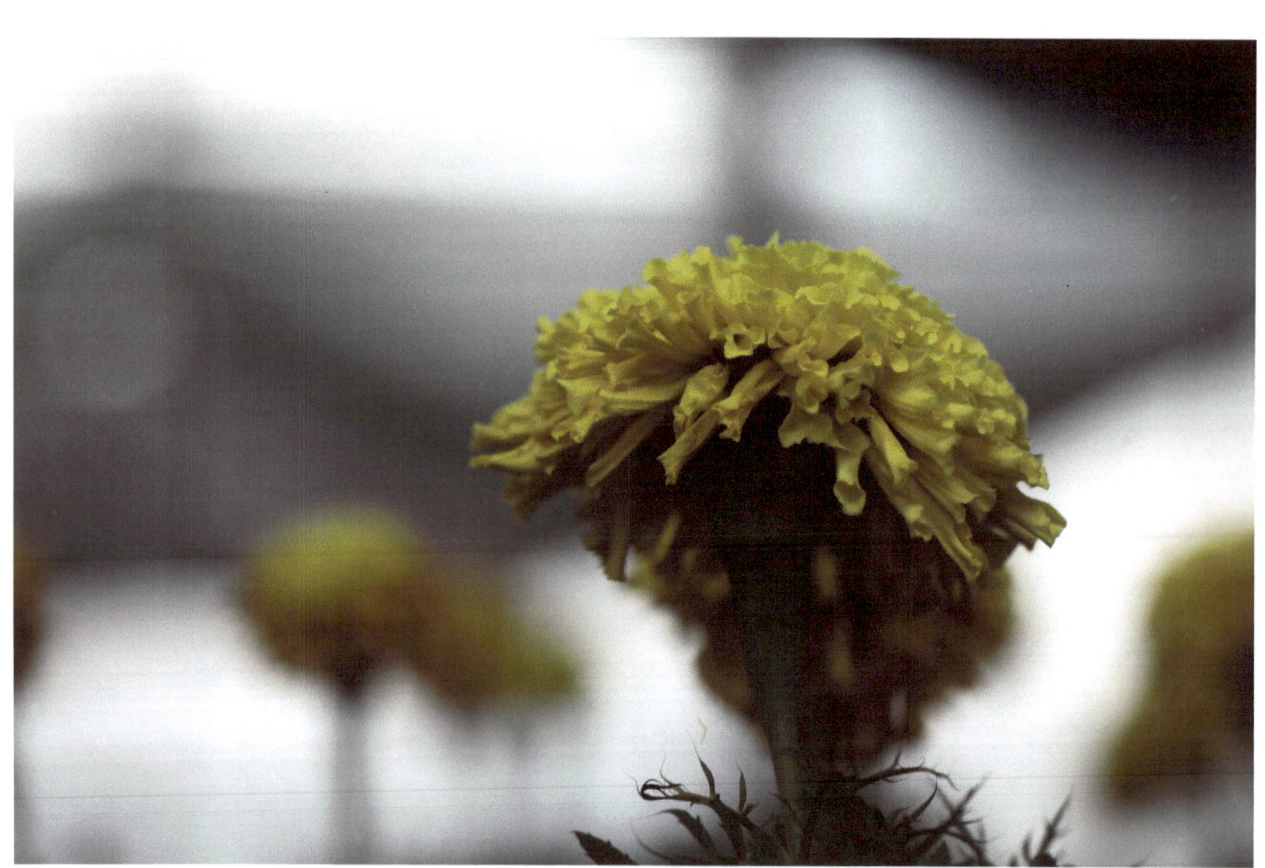

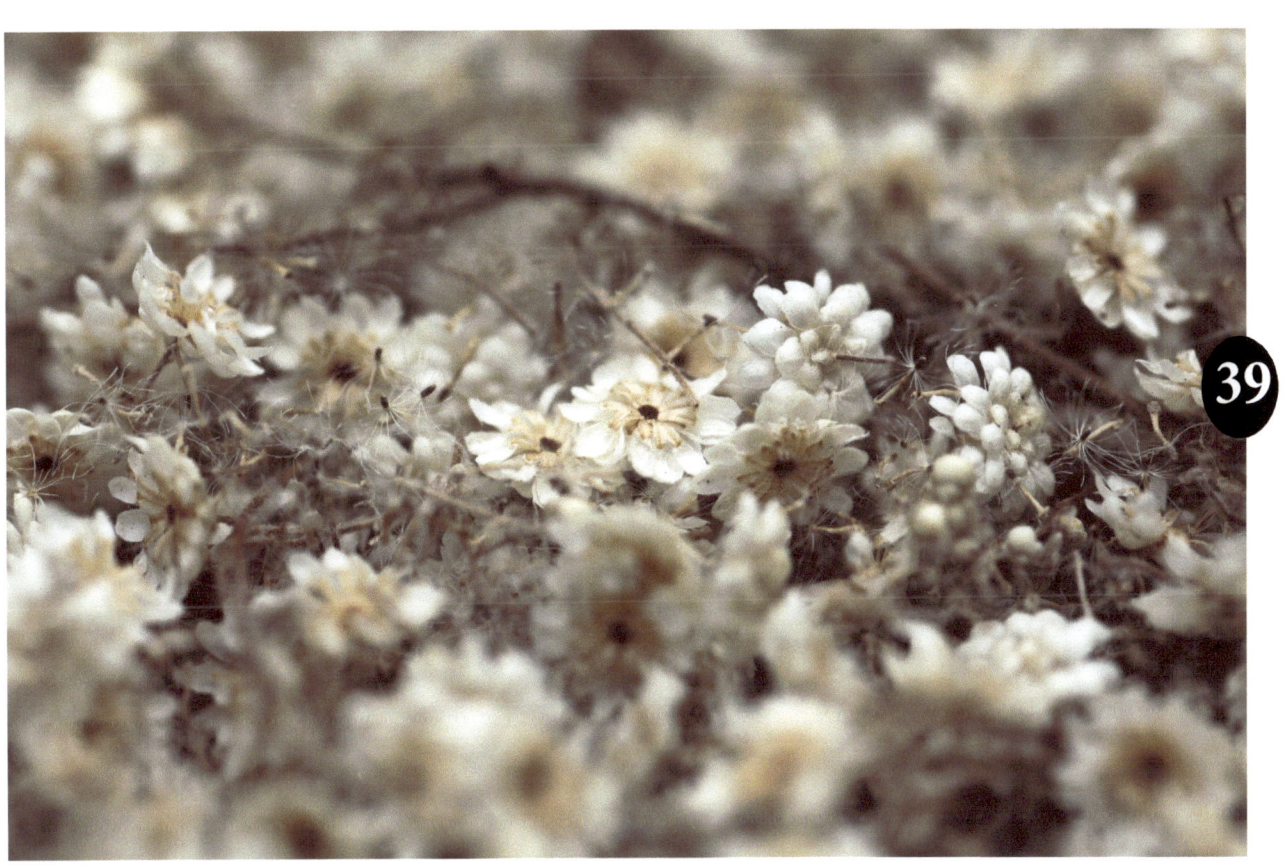

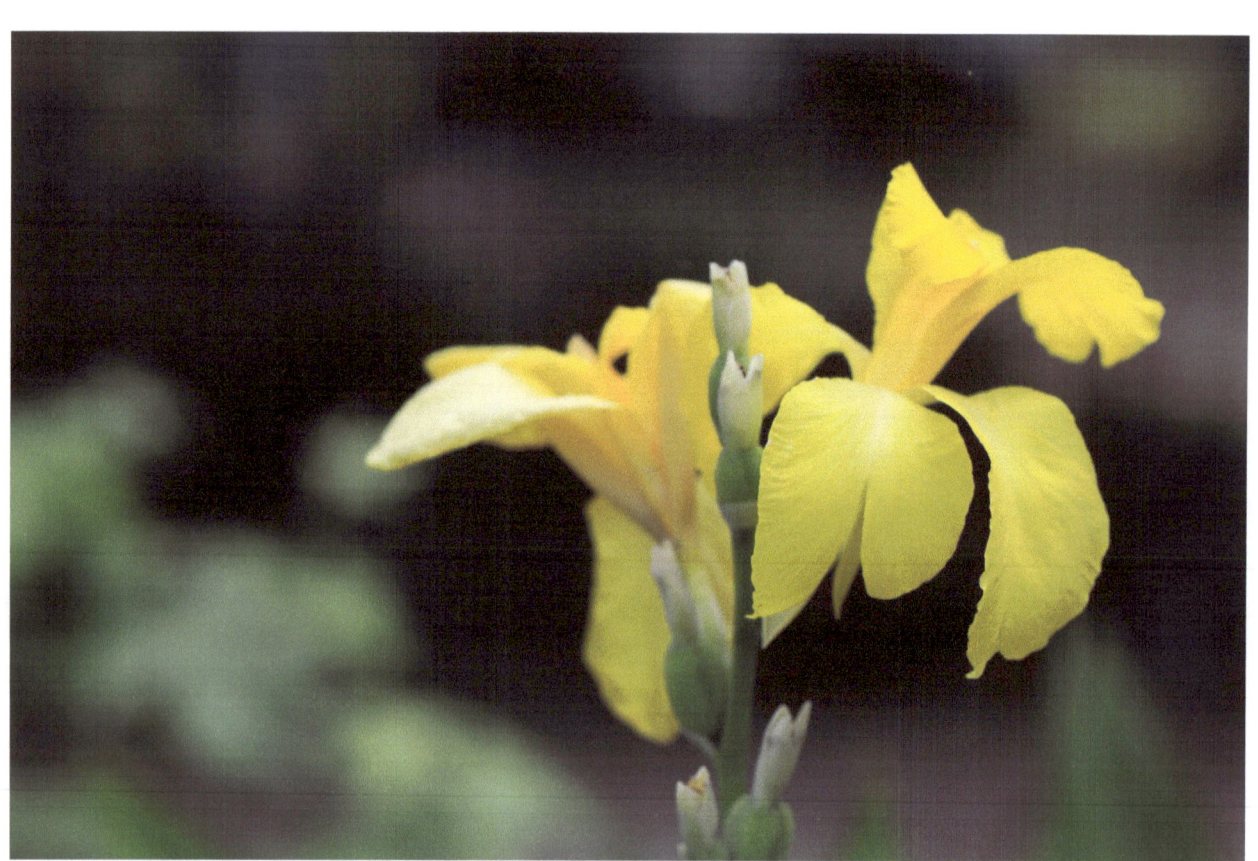

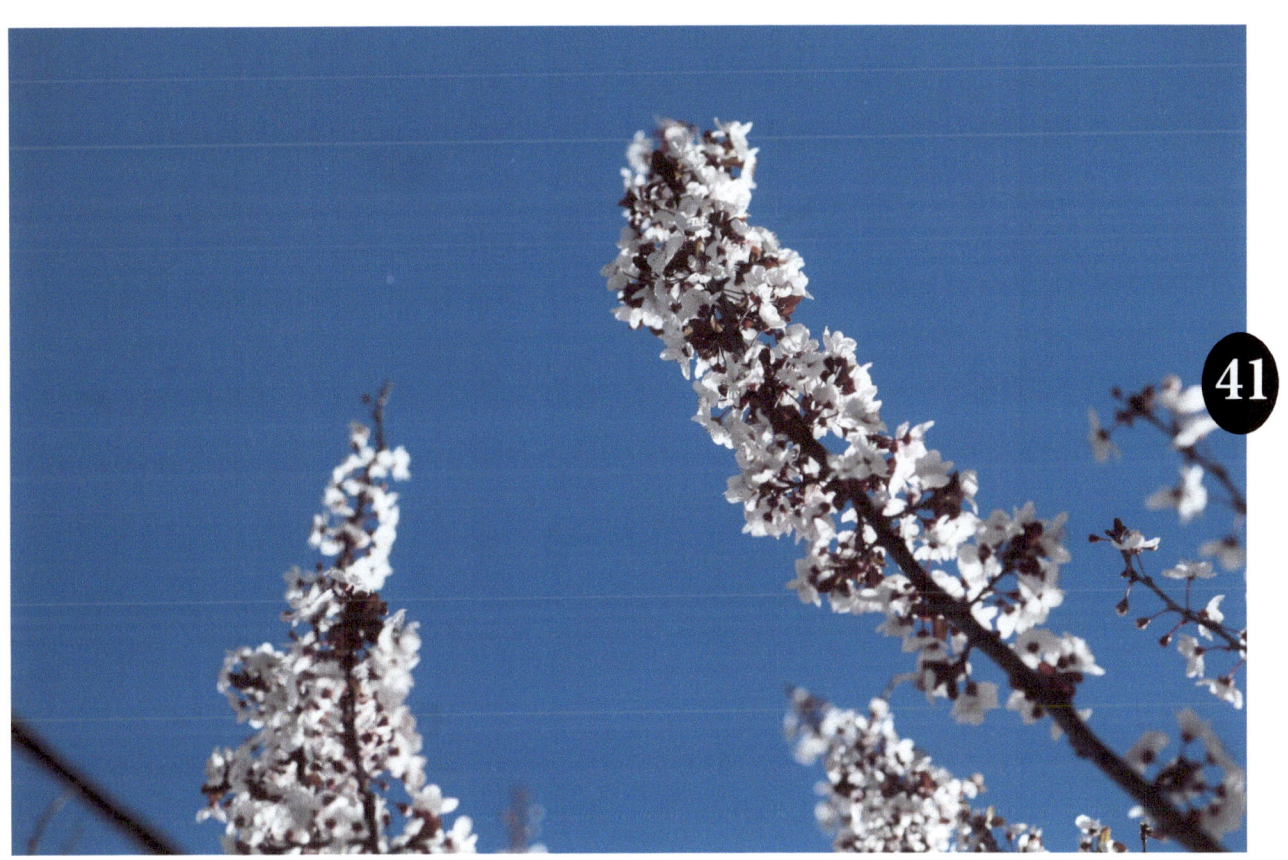

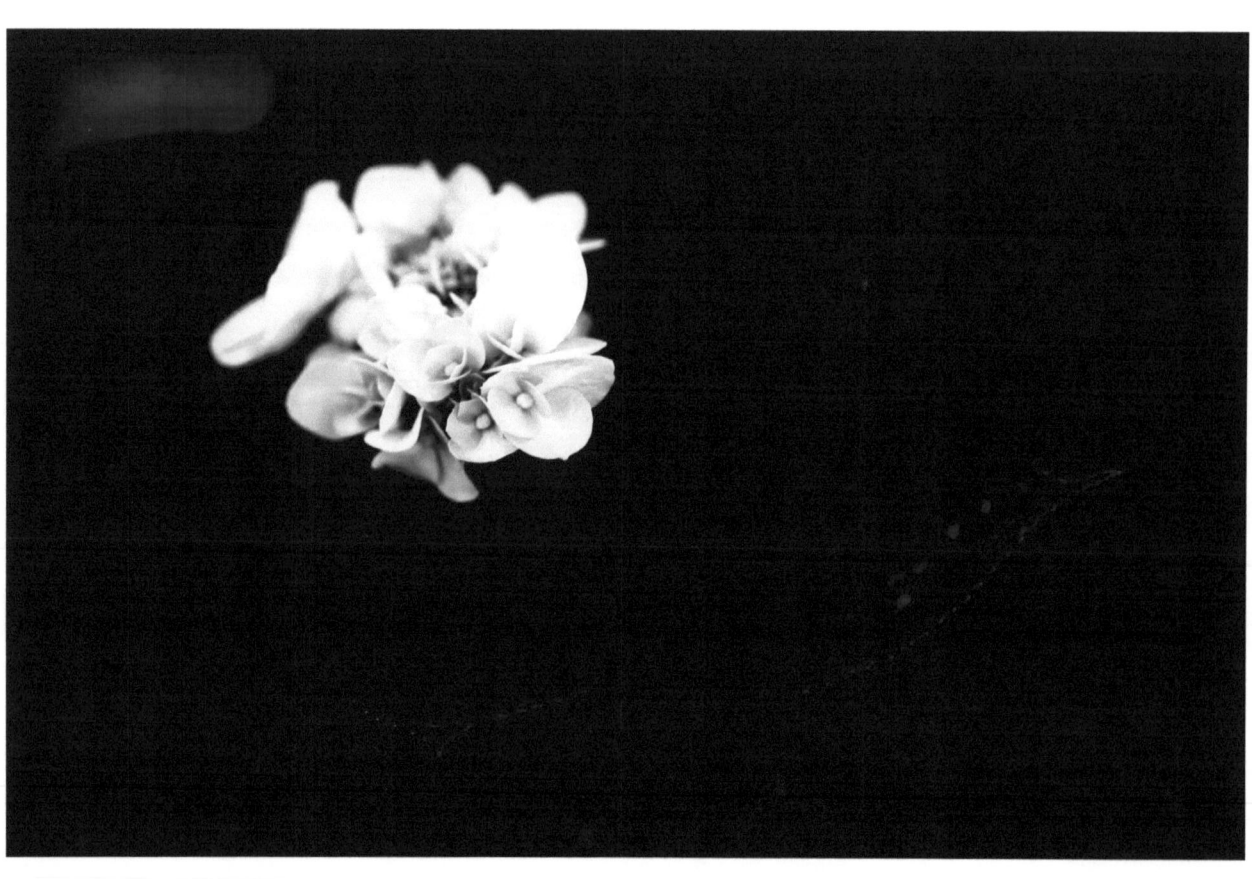

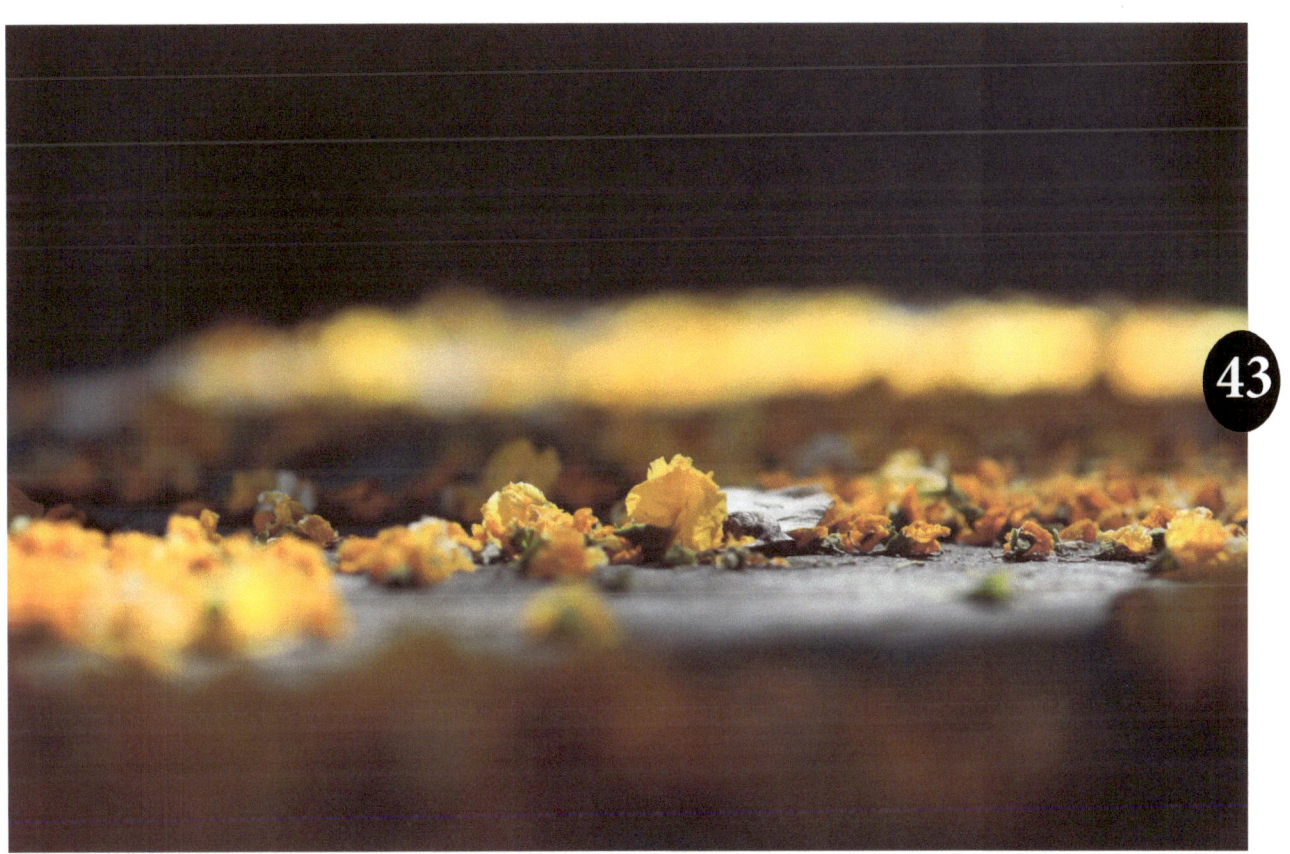

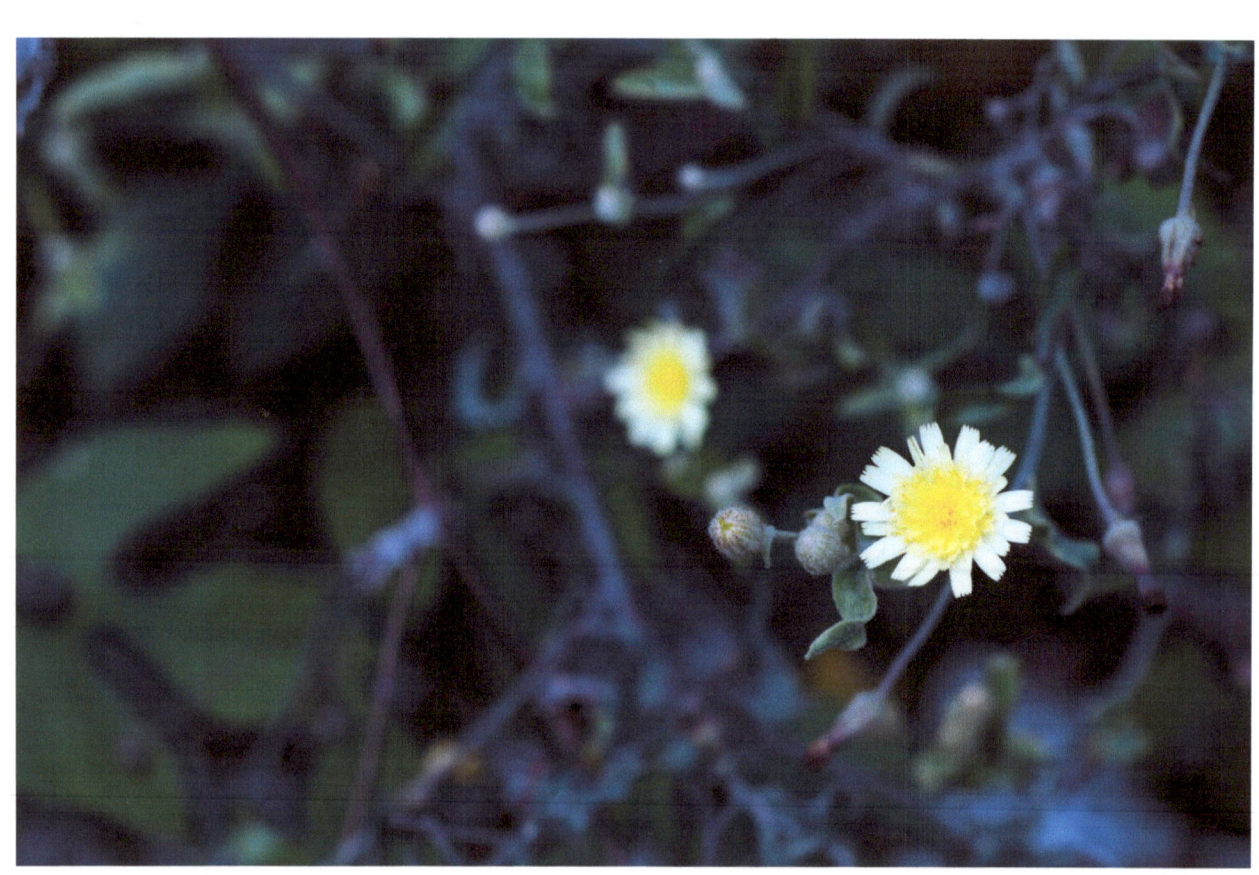

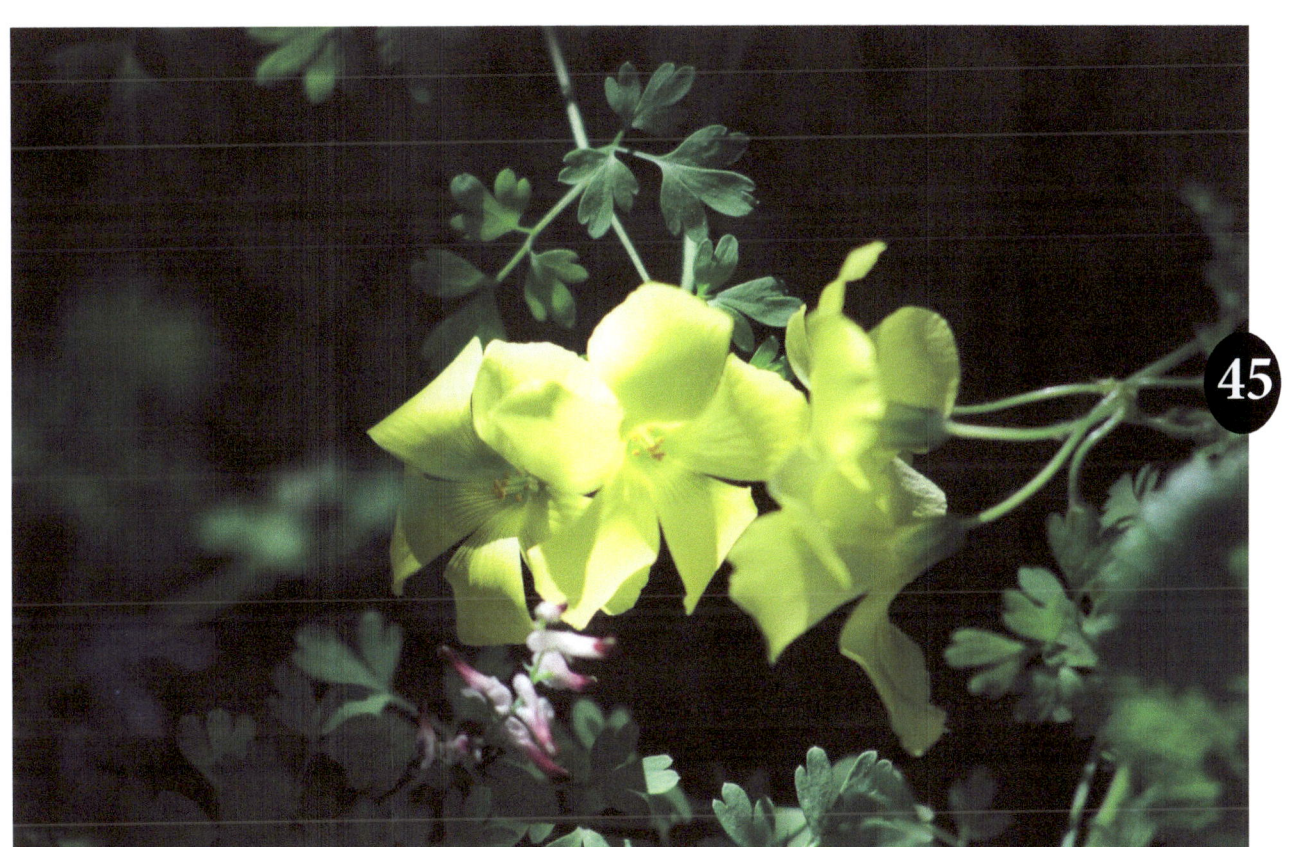

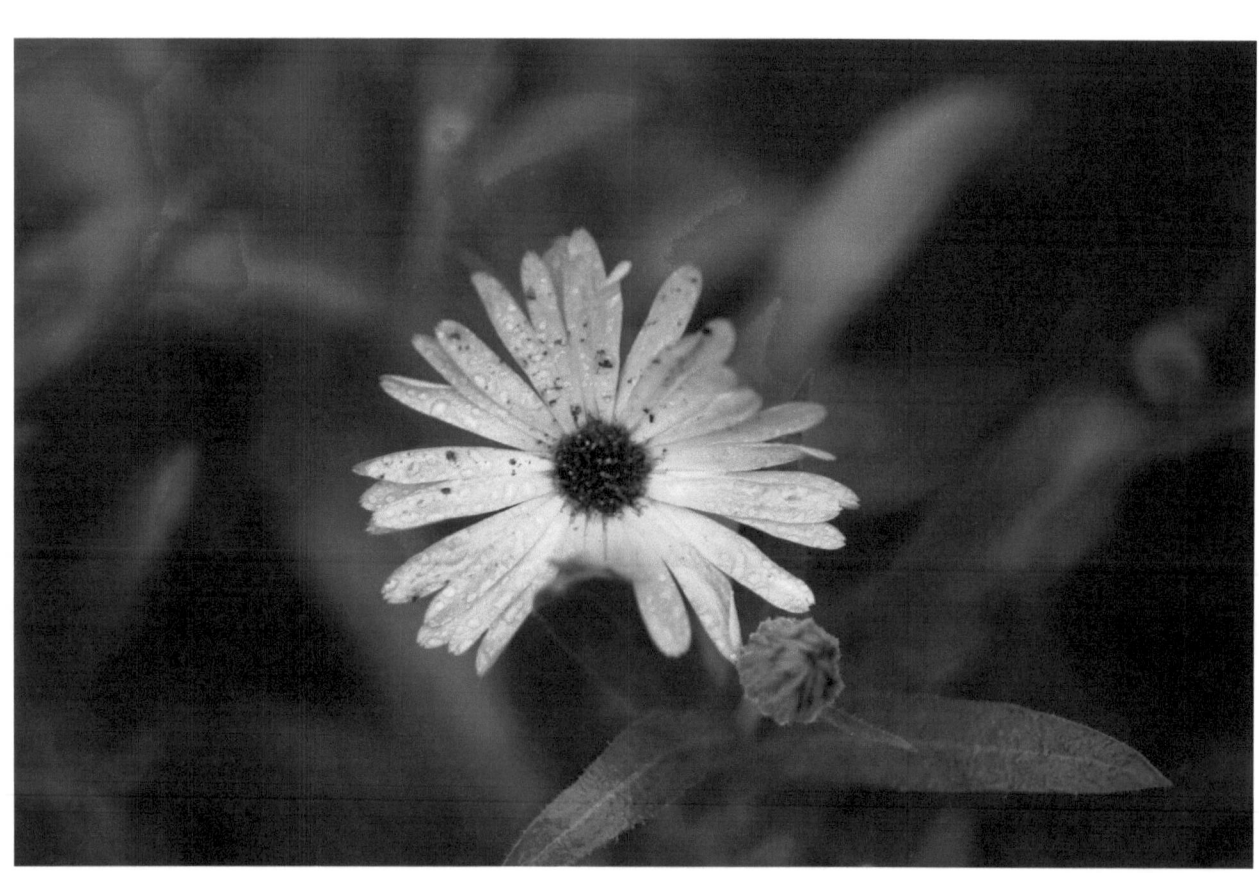

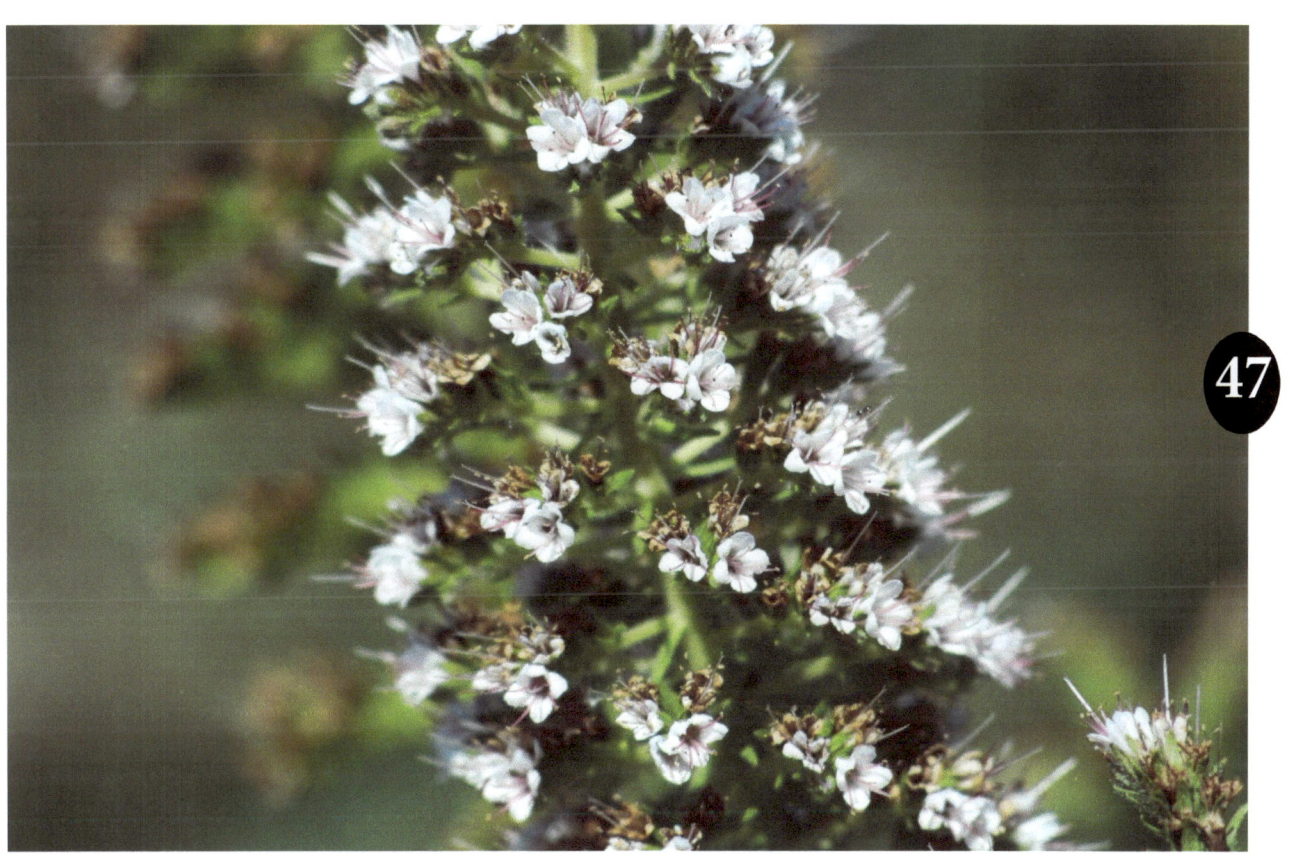

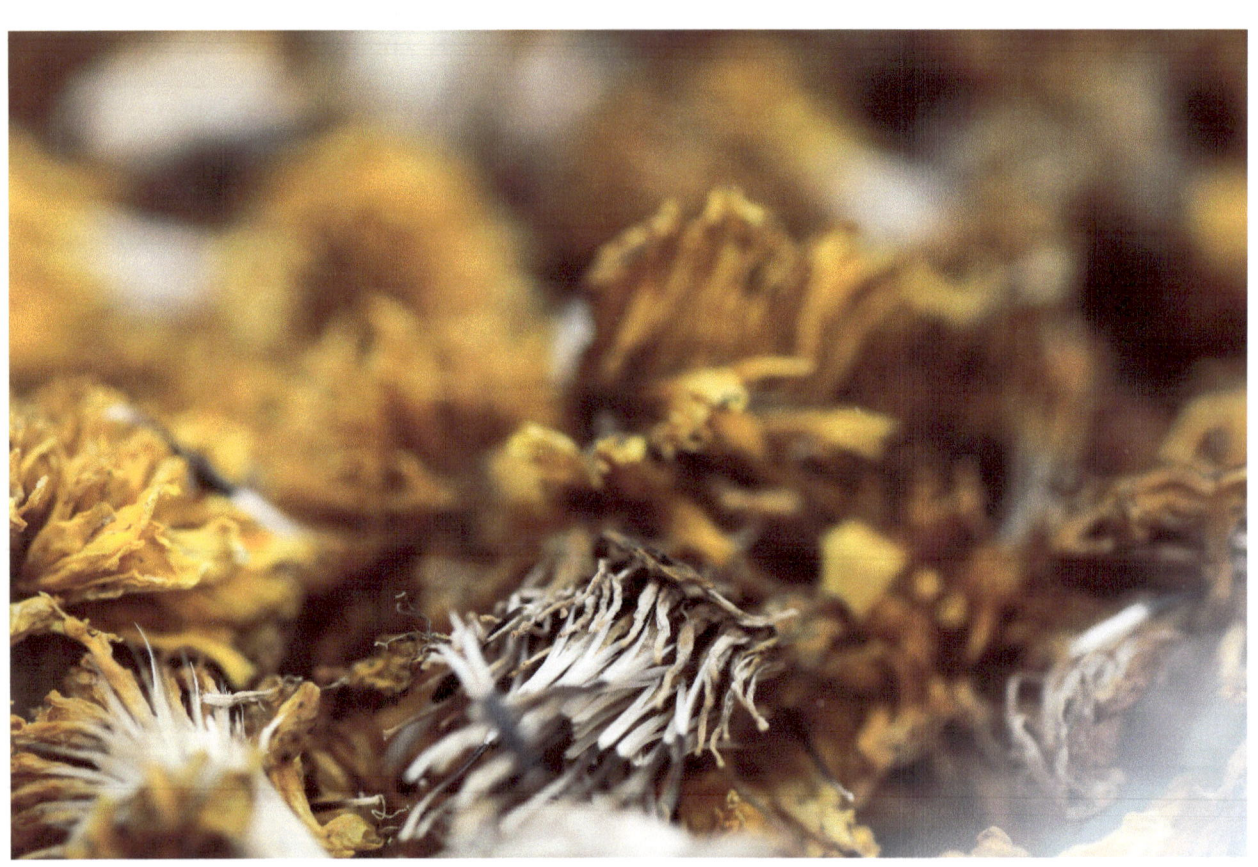

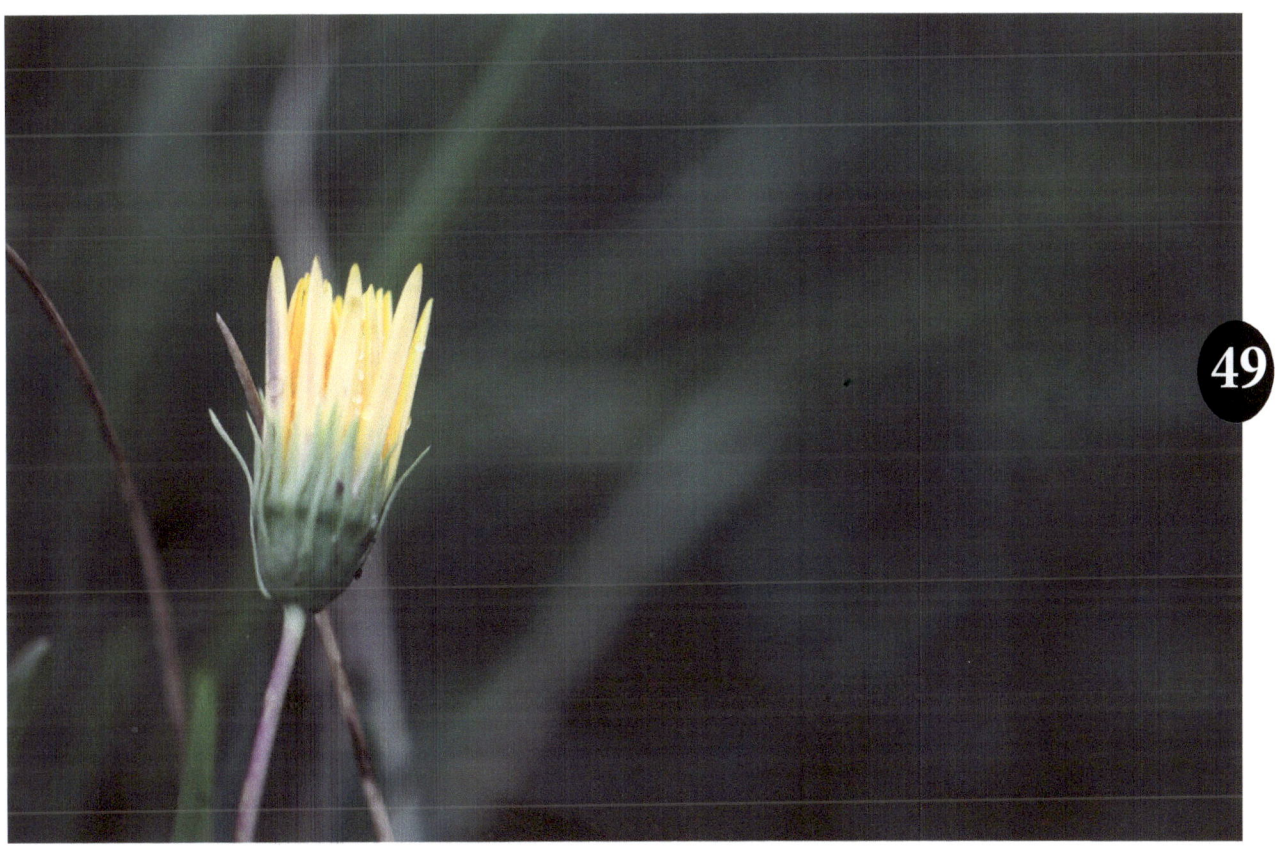

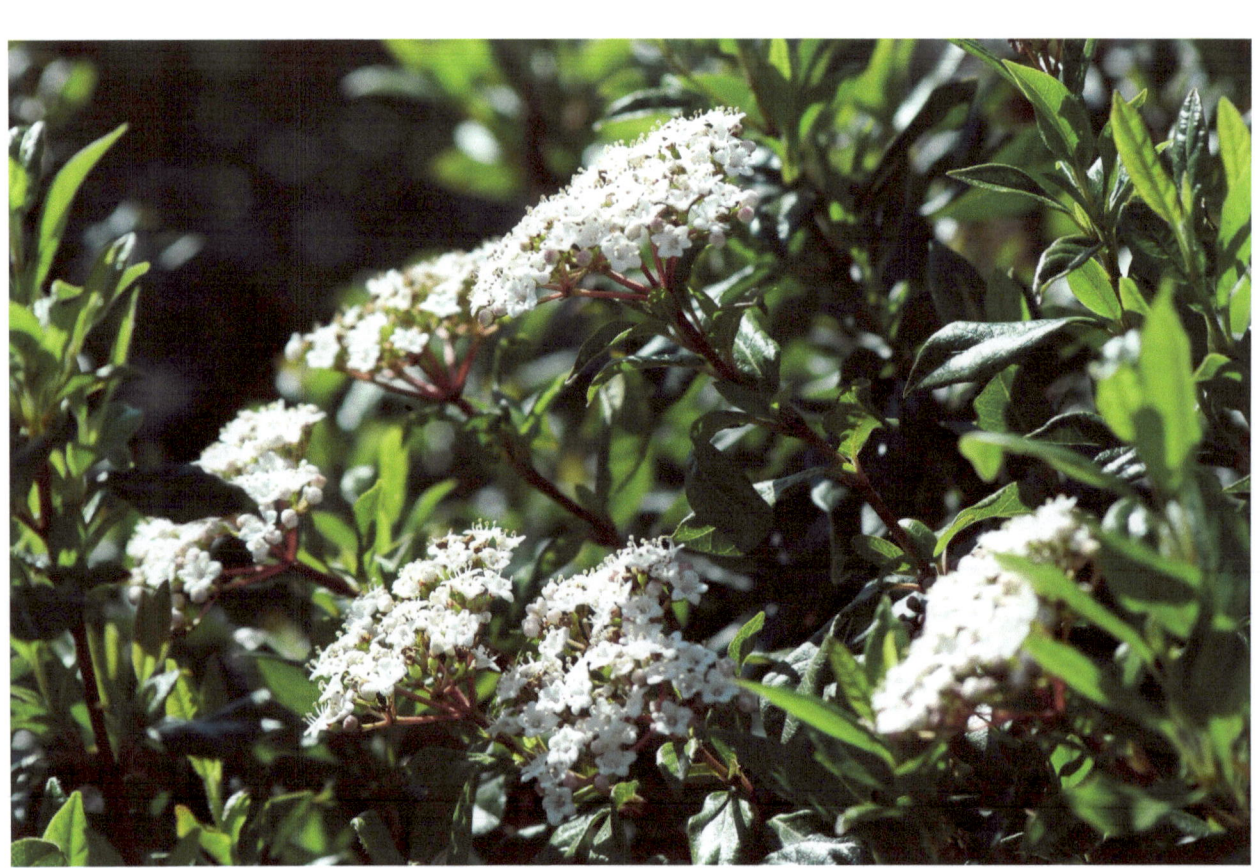

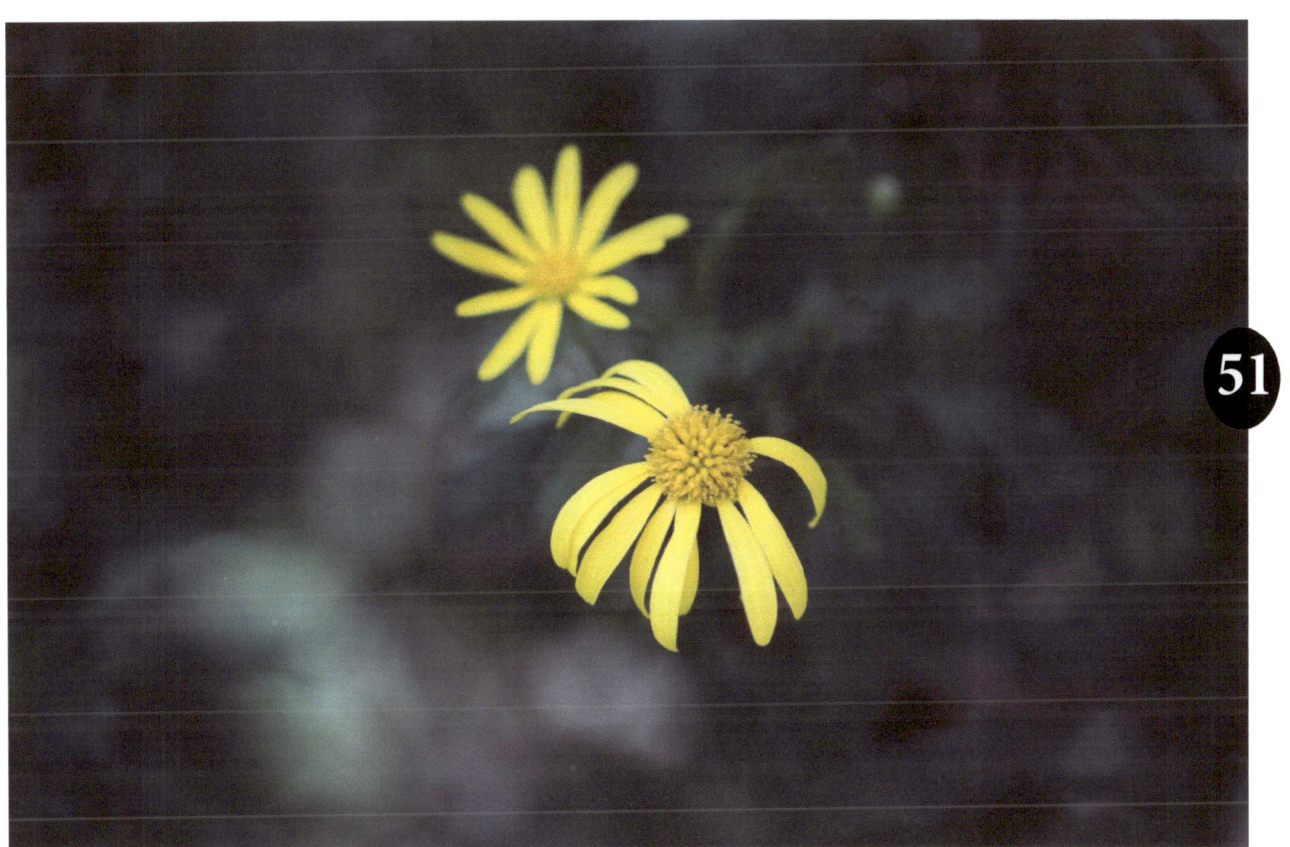

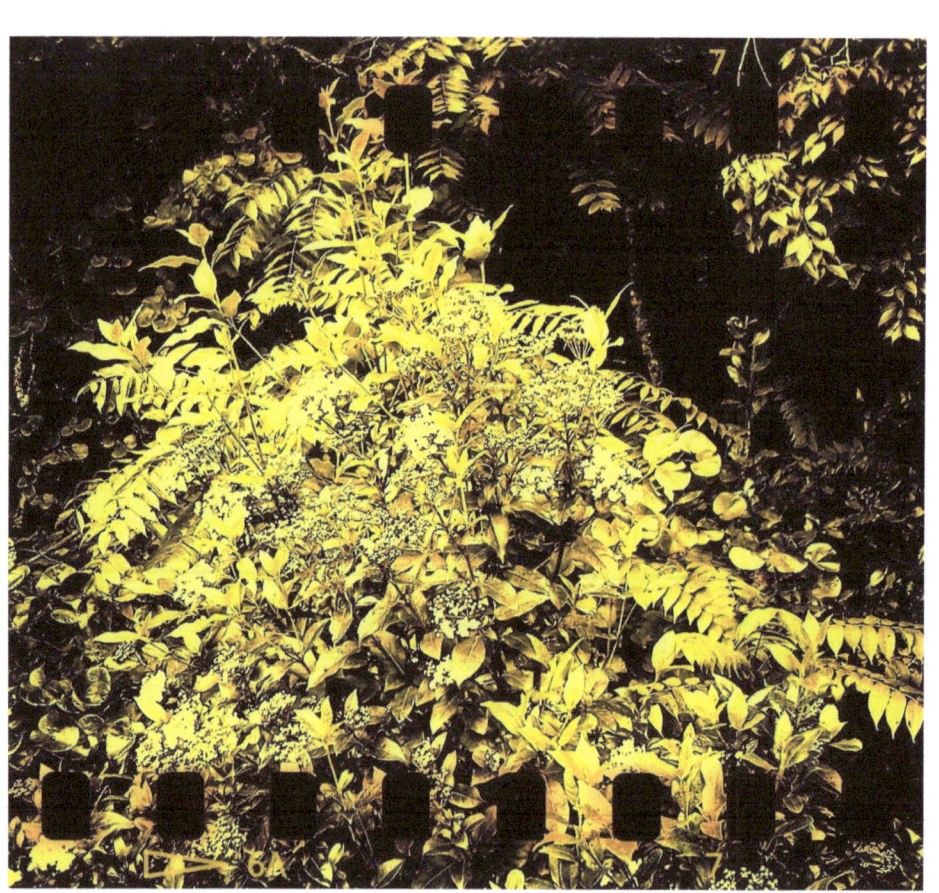

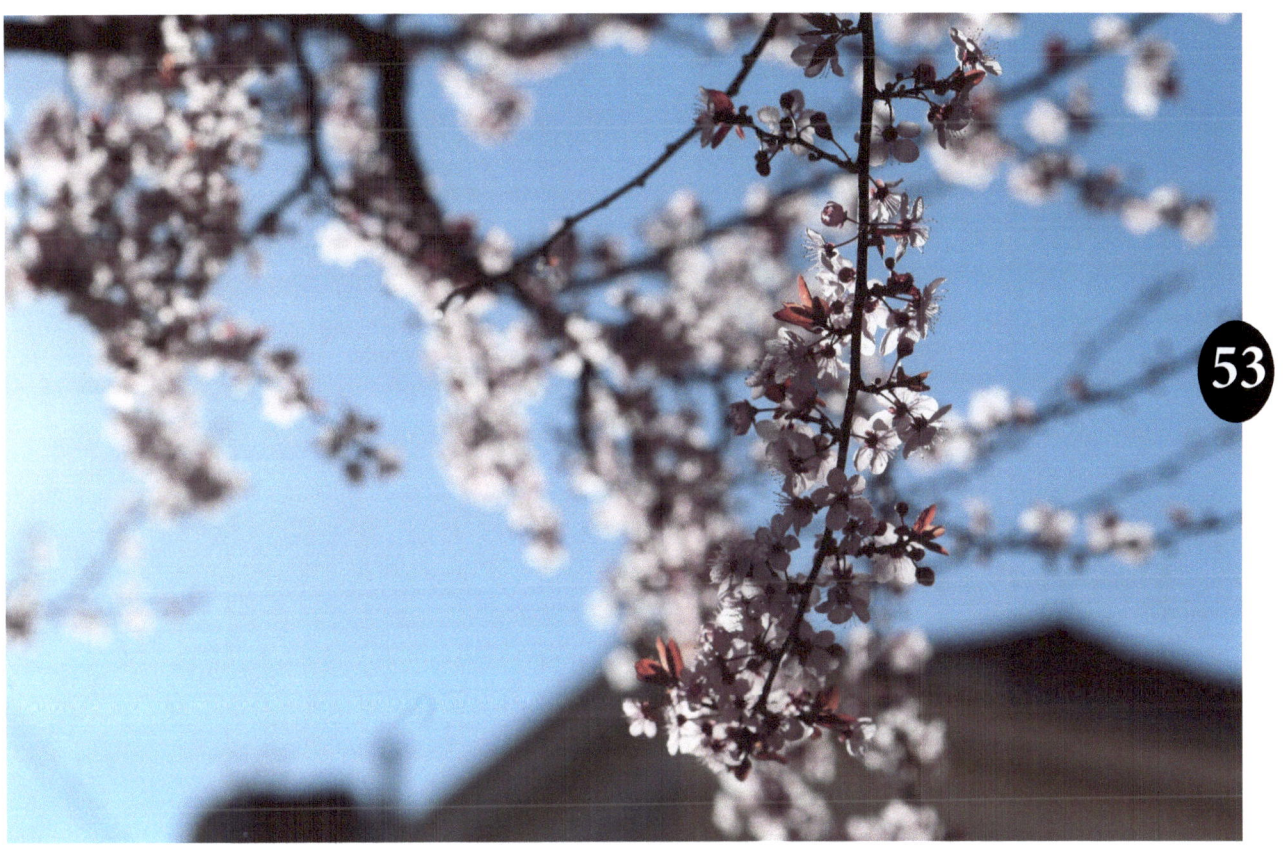

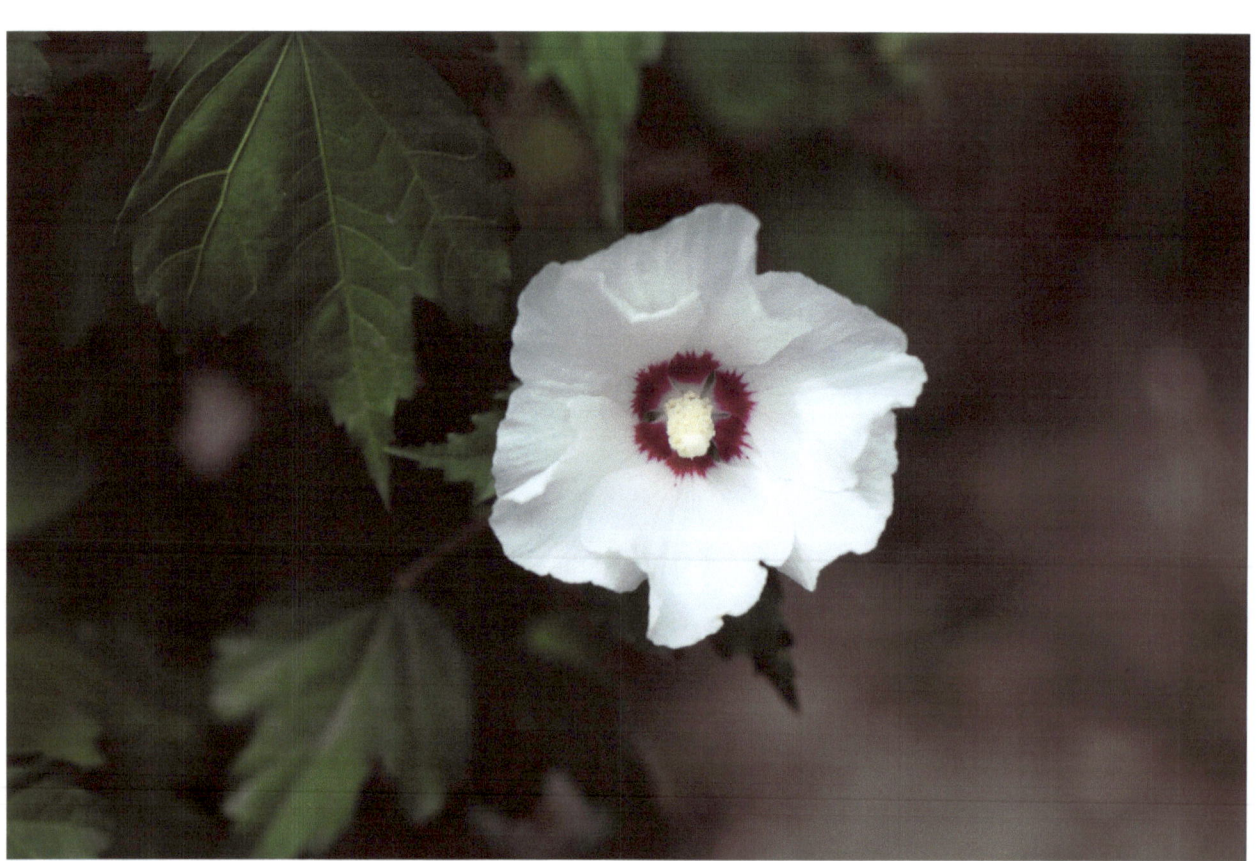

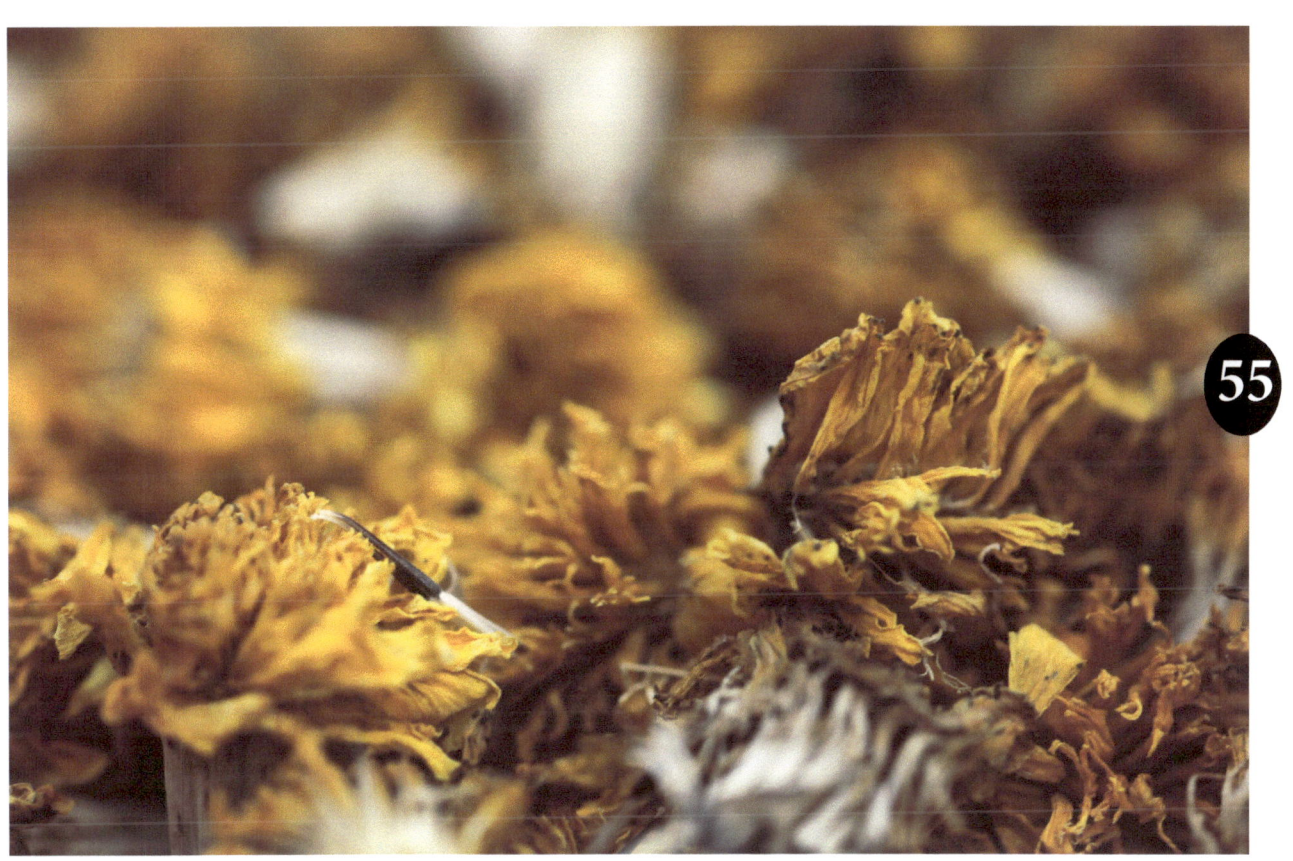

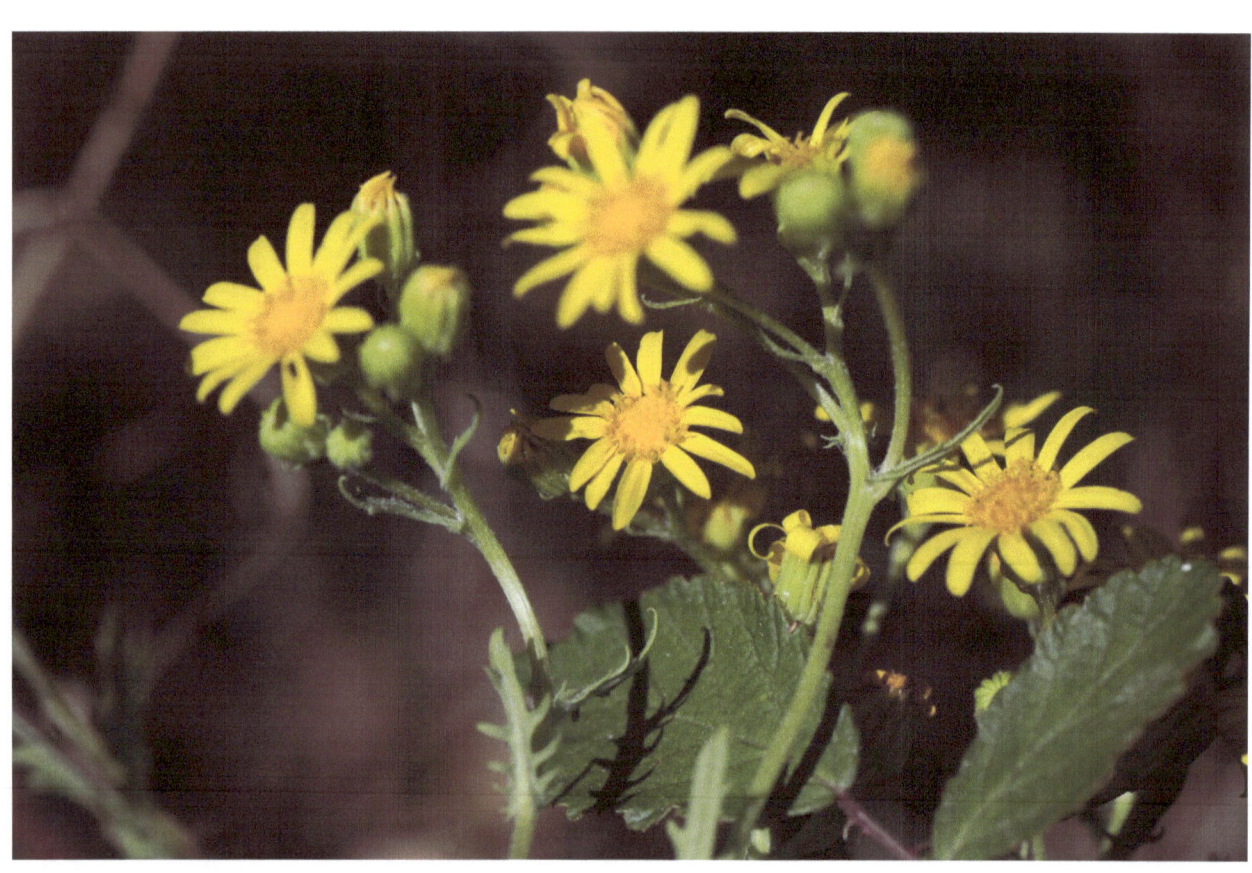

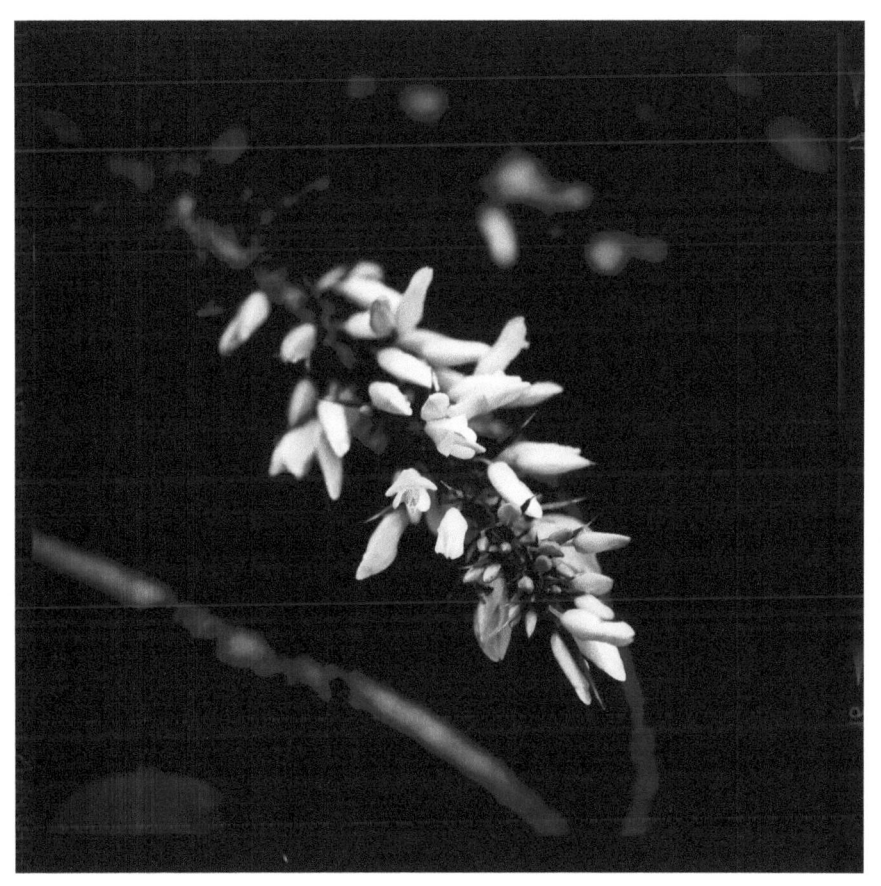

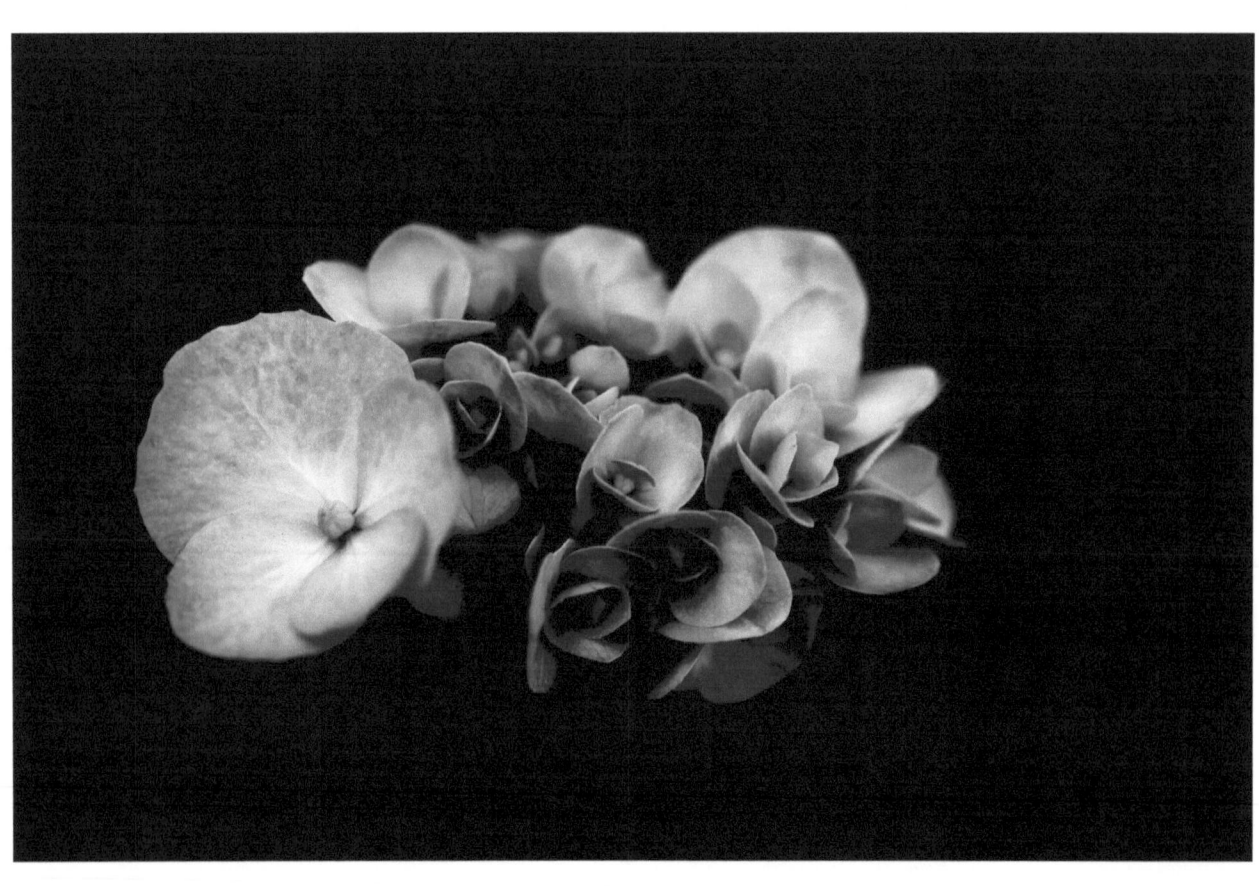

www.ingramcontent.com/pod-product-compliance
Lightning Source LLC
Chambersburg PA
CBHW051209220526
45473CB00003B/963